How To Manage Your Paperwork

A Simple and Practical Record Keeping System for Individuals, Homes, and Small Businesses

Charles Bradley

Hill Springs Publications

5023 Kentucky Street
South Charleston, West Virginia 25309

"Knowledge can govern destiny."

"Good order is the foundation of all good things."

Library of Congress Cataloging-in-Publication Data

Bradley, Charles.
  How to manage your paperwork.

  Bibliography: p.
  Includes index.
  1. Paperwork (Office practice)--Management. I. Title.
HF5547.15.B72 1988   651.5   87-35593
ISBN 0-931856-07-8

First Edition

Second Printing

Printed in the United States of America

Bradley, Charles
HOW TO MANAGE YOUR PAPERWORK - A Simple And Practical Record
Keeping System For Individuals, Homes, And Small Businesses

Includes List of Illustrations, Glossary, Index, and
Bibliography.

ISBN 0-931856-07-8

Published by
Hill Springs Publications (SAN 211-5735)
5023 Kentucky Street
South Charleston, WV 25309-1213

To Patti — whose mountain of papers
and encouragement inspired this book.

Other books by Charles (Jack) Bradley

- - -

How To Read & Write Music,
Including Professional Chord Symbol Method

How To Tune, Repair, and Regulate Pianos
A Practical Guide - Illustrated

How To Read, Write, and Understand Music
A Practical Guide - Illustrated

Contents

List Of Illustrations   10

About This Book   11

SECTION 1. A PLAN OF ATTACK   13

    The Paper Monster
    Like Falling Snow
    A Plan
    Setting Up Your Command Center
    Set A Time
    Knowledge Is Power
    Keeping Records
    Why Keep Records?
    Some Basic Definitions

SECTION 2. A SORTING PLAN   20

    To Keep Or Not To Keep
    What You Will Need
    From What Date To What Date?
    What The IRS Says
    Sorting
    Item-Type Sorting
    Item-Type Sorting List
    Item-Date Sorting
    Keeping Important Documents

SECTION 3. A FILING PLAN   29

    Filing
    Business Depends On Filing
    Example Of A Business Filing System
    Eleven Steps
    Some Filing Basics
    Captions
    More Screening
    Using Filing Cabinets Or Boxes?
    Protecting Your Records
    Using The File Folders And Envelopes

SECTION 4. HOW TO FILE   39

    A Brief Explanation
    Indexing
    Terms For Indexing
    Names In Their Natural Order

The Same Names Transposed For Filing And Alphabetized
More Names
The Same Names Transposed For Filing And Alphabetized
The Rules For Filing
Rule 1. Names Of Individuals
Rule 2. In Alphabetic Order
Rule 3. Surname Alone Or With Initial
Rule 4. Prefixes To Surnames
Rule 5. Company Or Firm Names
Rule 6. Complete Individual Names Within Firm Names
Rule 7. Abbreviations
Rule 8. The Article "The"
Rule 9. Names That Are Hyphenated
Rule 10. Prepositions, Conjunctions, And Company
          Name Endings

SECTION 5. SETTING UP YOUR FILING SYSTEM   48

    Putting It All Together
    Reminder List
    Appliance Manuals
    Purging Your Files

SECTION 6. CHECKING ACCOUNTS AND CHECK REGISTERS   51

    Some Banking Definitions
    Identifying Accounts
    Differences In Check Registers
    Other Types Of Check Registers
    Refinements To The Ledger-Type Check Register
    Balancing Your Checkbook
    Account Reconciliation

SECTION 7. LEDGER BOOKS   57

    What You Will Need
    Where To Find These Items
    Manufacturers of Ledger Books And Pads
    Using The ledger Books
    Setting Up The Columns
    Suggestions For Groupings
    Suggested Columns

SECTION 8. ENTERING YOUR FILES IN THE LEDGERS   65

    Dividing Up The Pages
    Writing In The Ledger Spaces
    Putting In The Column Headings
    Making Some Entries
    Insurance Due Dates

SECTION 9. WRAPPING UP THE SYSTEM   82

Labeling The ledger Books
Three- And Four-Column Check Register Pages
Comment About Computers
Adding The Columns
Earnings Record
Protecting Your Books
Congratulations

SECTION 10. SMALL BUSINESS APPLICATION   92

Different Needs
Reasons For A Record Keeping System
Easy To Use
What You Need To Keep Track Of
Customer Sales
The Importance Of A Customer List
Many Kinds Of Systems
Methods For Income And Expenses
Your Checkbook
Check Ledgers
The Cash Receipt Book
Expenditures Book
Credit Card Purchases
Travel Expenses
Keep Records Up To Date
Making Entries
The Customer Order Book
Purchasing
Hints And Helps
Paper Intimidation
"Do We Need This?"
Phone Calls And Notes Versus Letters
Ease At Tax Time
Guidelines and Axioms

SECTION 11. SOME OTHER USES FOR THIS SYSTEM   113

Inventory Records
Keeping Track Of Your Investments
Health-Related
Financial Obligations
Ideas And Inventions
About The Author

Glossary   121

Index   125

Bibliography   127

List Of Illustrations

File-folders   36

File drawer and file box   37

File cabinets   38

Pocket check registers   53

Ledger check register   54

Account reconciliation form   56

Samples of ledger pages   62, 63, 64

"Individual" ledger column headings   68, 69

"Home-related" ledger column headings   70, 71

"Child", "Auto", and misc. ledger column headings   71, 72

"Individual" Insurance and Medical ledger   74, 75

"Individual" Personal and Self-improvement ledger   76, 77

"Home-related" expense ledgers   78, 79, 80, 81

Three-column check register page   83

Four-column check register page   84

Ledger pages showing totals   86

Pages showing earnings record   88, 89

A four-column check register   97

Entries in a cash receipt book   98

Expenditure Book entries   100, 101

Customer Order Book entries   104, 105

Sample of an inventory record   114

Investment record and tracking sheets   116, 117

+-+-+-+-+-+-+-+-+-+-+

About This Book

Possibly the reason you are looking at or reading this book is because your "papers" are in a hopeless mess. If that is so, you are looking in the right place. This book will show you how to solve that problem and to prevent it from ever overtaking you again. Read on.

The purpose of this book is to provide the average individual, householder, or owner of a small business, with a simple, practical, and inexpensive system of keeping records. Not only for tax purposes, but as a means of logging in income, expenses, insurance premiums (and dates due), medical expenses, business expenses, etc. in a quick and easy system that puts all necessary information at your fingertips - and all **without a computer.**

There is a concept that "order gets order." If you have your papers and records in good order, a feeling of harmony will travel over into other sectors of your life and inspire an improved self-image and a feeling of accomplishment and being in control. This alone is well worth the effort of putting this system to use.

Two methods are offered here: One with and one without filing cabinets. This choice depends much on the size of your paper problem or business operation - both methods are inexpensive.

This book does not attempt to compete with computer database programs. It is primarily for low-volume record keeping. In its own way it is more convenient, more flexible, and most certainly, much less expensive to set up and operate.

If portions of the text in this book seem overly simplistic to some, it is because the author wrote with the assumption that some readers may have little or no knowledge of the subjects involved.

By following the methods laid out in this book, the reader will be able to establish or restore order regarding their personal or small business paperwork. And when tax time comes around, scrambling through stacks of papers and piles of slips will be a thing of the past. Simply add up a few columns and the answers are yours.

This book could be one of the smartest purchases of your lifetime.

+-+-+-+-+-+-+-+

Section 1. A Plan Of Attack

THE PAPER MONSTER

Since writing was invented by the Sumarians about 3100 BC, man has used it to communicate and record information for future use. In recent years we have rapidly become an "information society" with the ever increasing importance of data accessibility. Even with the advent of the computer age, paperwork for the average individual has greatly increased.

Day-to-day living is becoming more complex and documentation more a part of our lives. Taxes must be paid, insurance, mortgages, loans and utility payments must be made on time. A record of deductibles and other items must be kept.

If some system is not established to cope with this ever-increasing deluge of papers, one day a person discovers that his business affairs are in complete disarray and there is a "paper monster" preparing to tear his world to shreds.

The simple systems described in this book will enable any person who can read and write to get his business and financial records in order - and keep them that way. At a glance, the user can determine what is owed, when payment is due, and how much money he has, etc. And when tax time comes around, fumbling with piles of papers and receipts is a thing of the past. Just add a few columns of figures with a calculator and the information you need is at your fingertips.

This book can save you hours of drudgery and mental anguish with your personal business (and small business) papers accumulation. Once this system is put to use, it is almost a pleasure to make entries and to know at a glance the condition of your affairs. And more important, using this system can prevent many serious problems arising from forgetfulness or neglect because of piled-up and disorderly papers. Begin learning and using this simple system now. Banish the "paper monster" forever, then relax.

LIKE FALLING SNOW

Each day the mail brings more paper: advertisements, bills, letters, notices and solicitations from all manner of sources. Most of this, of course, is of little immediate interest and is tossed in "File 13", the wastebasket. But what remains, papers that demand or require attention, and some things that appear interesting and suggest another look later, have a way of piling up.

Without a system it isn't long until the constant snowfall of papers has grown to a formidable jumble and there is a strong temptation to throw out the whole thing. But obviously, such drastic action could later cause some serious problems.

A PLAN

Unless you are wealthy enough to have a personal accountant, the only realistic answer to this ever growing problem is to have some plan of action and to use it regularly - and that is what this book is all about. It will show you how to sort your present and future accumulations of papers and decide which to keep and which to throw away. It will then show you how to separate your papers into categories, set up a record system and record the proper information from your papers. It will then show you how to file your papers for future reference, if the need to retrieve them should arise.

SETTING UP YOUR COMMAND CENTER

Decide on a place where at least once a week you can sort and process your important papers. This should be a large, flat surface such as a kitchen or dining area table, a card table, or any similar surface that is hard and flat and has enough space for a work surface. A desk would be ideal.

If possible, have your "office" in a place away from heavy people traffic where you can concentrate without frequent interruptions. Suitable light should be provided by having it near a window or by using desk-lamp or other lamp.

SET A TIME

Of course the best remedy is prevention. After you clear up your original hill of papers (which will be explained in detail later), set a time each week to process the current accumulation. And of course if you have a small business, more frequent sessions would be called for.

The important thing is to set a time on a certain day of the week and regardless of distractions, use this time strictly for paperwork. After doing this a few times and the habit has been formed, regular processing sessions will seem like the natural thing to do.

You can keep the value and importance of these sessions in mind if you think of the mess and frustration that existed before using a regular system.

KNOWLEDGE IS POWER

In the business sector, creative salesmanship, intense competition, and clever innovation are often sighted as the reason millions of consumer demands can be translated into billions of dollars worth of products and services. However, much of the answer lies in the fact that business has made more effective use of records than ever before in history.

Since keeping good records is so effective in the business sector, a scaled-down, proportionate system is equally effective with the individual.

WHY KEEP RECORDS?

Without records any business operation would soon come to a chaotic standstill. All businesses need and use various record systems in order to know: how much money they are making (or losing), what is their inventory, their needs for the future, the number of their employees and their salaries and taxes, the company's operating expenses, taxes, and so on.

Think of yourself as a small business or corporation. You are your only employee, yet you need to keep the same basic records as a small company would - just not as many.

You should keep records of your income, business related expenses, living expenses, insurance and medical expenses, etc. etc. By knowing what you earn and what you spend, you will have a much clearer picture of what your resources really are and how you can improve them. Suppose you are spending more than you are earning. With records you can see at a glance where your money is going and what can be cut back to prevent this certain and eventual disaster.

Suppose something happens to your job. If you have kept records of your living expenses and kept your bank account balanced, you can know in a few seconds just how long you can hang on before finding another job becomes imperative.

SOME BASIC DEFINITIONS

To contribute to his general knowledge, whether he intends to make a career in the financial world or not, every intelligent adult should have an every-day knowledge of some of the basic financial terms and procedures. This will also help dispel some of the aura of mystery that seems to naturally surround money and help the individual approach money with a more practical, rather than a romantic view.

There is a glossary of terms in the back of this book, but here are a few definitions to break the ice.

account - A record or similar monetary transactions.

Accounting - The system of analysis and interpretation of the financial and bookkeeping records of an enterprise, used to evaluate the progress or failure of a business, and to recognize the factors that indicate its true condition.

accrue - To grow or accumulate, as the interest earned on money.

balance - Equality between the debit and credit sides of an account.

Balance Sheet - A statement of the financial conditions of a business at a certain date, showing its assets, liabilities and capitol.

bookkeeping - The recording of the accounts and transactions of a business.

corporation - A legal entity, chartered by a U.S. state or the federal government, and separate and distinct from the persons who own it.

credit - In bookkeeping: The entry of any amount paid by a debtor.

debit - An item of debt recorded in an account, or the sum of several such entries.

equity: The money value of, or the interest in a property in excess of claims or liens against it.

interest - Payment for the use of money or credit, usually a percentage of the amount owed.

mortgage - A transfer of property pledges as security for the repayment of a loan.

profit - Excess of returns over outlay or expenditure. What is left after all costs and expenses are paid.

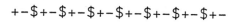

Section 2. A Sorting Plan

TO KEEP OR NOT TO KEEP

Usually, the toughest part of any task is the decision making. First there is the decision to recognize the problem, then there is the decision to take action. After these initial steps have been taken, only the <u>how</u> remains. This section will show you the how.

WHAT YOU WILL NEED

Acquire several medium size cardboard boxes from your local supermarket, or most any business establishment that receives its stock in cardboard containers. The number of boxes you will need depends on the size of your paper accumulation. For the average problem, however, acquire four medium size boxes and a large wastebasket. You will also need some rubber bands and a few dozen brown envelopes, slightly larger than #10 business size, or approximately 11" X 4-1/2" or 5". These can be found at department or variety stores and office supply stores.

FROM WHAT DATE TO WHAT DATE?

If your papers have been piling up for years, this may take a little longer to straighten out - but don't despair; this system works just as well with old papers as new ones.

Since only you know your exact needs, only you can decide on how far back you care to keep old papers. The following excerpts form an IRS publication will help you decide what and how far back to keep papers.

WHAT THE IRS SAYS

From: "Your Federal Income Tax Return" (1986 edition).

"... You must keep records so that you can prepare a complete and accurate income tax return. The law does not require any special form of records. However, you should keep all receipts, canceled checks, and other evidence to prove amounts you claim as deductions or credits.

If you file a claim for refund, you must be able to prove by your records that you have overpaid your tax.

You must keep your records for as long as they are important for any Internal Revenue law.

Keep records that support an item of income or a deduction appearing on a return until the statute of limitations for the return runs out. Usually this is 3 years from the date the return was due or filed, or 2 years from the date the tax was paid, whichever date is later. However, sometimes you may have to keep records for a longer period of time. For example, if you income average you may need to prove your taxable income for the base period years.

In property transactions, sometimes the basis of new or replacement property depends on the basis of the old property.

Keep the records of the transactions relating to the basis of property for as long as they are important in figuring the basis of the original or replacement property.

Sometimes new laws give benefits to taxpayers who can prove from their records from previous years that they are entitled to such benefits.

Keep copies of the returns you have filed and the tax return package as part of your records. They may be helpful in amending filed returns or preparing future ones. ..."

SORTING

Place the two boxes and the wastebasket near a large table or flat surface. Began on your pile(s) of papers and sort in the following manner:

In box #1, place papers to keep and process.

In box #2, put papers that will not go into your record books but are about things you may be interested in later and want to keep.

In the wastebasket, put papers such as old ads, circulars - things that are of no interest to you now. DO NOT throw away anything that you may need for a tax record or verification, such as wage records or paycheck stubs. Also receipts for items such as insurance, rent, utilities, etc. that you may have to produce in case of a dispute, etc.

ITEM-TYPE SORTING

Set the Number 2 box aside for perusal at your convenience. We will not be concerned with it anymore here. And of course, the papers in the wastebasket are considered expunged.

Take a handful of the papers from box Number 1 and begin sorting them in four piles: Personal, Children, Home-Related and Automobile. Of course if you do not have children or an automobile, you needn't bother with these items. Continue sorting until all of the items in Box Number 1 are sorted.

Next, sort the papers in each stack into other separate stacks, using the list below, adding or deleting items as you see fit, or make a list of your own that includes items for which you wish to keep records.

ITEM-TYPE SORTING LIST

INDIVIDUAL

Clothes	Investments
Contributions	Medical, Dental, Etc.
Insurance	Memberships
Education	Taxes
Entertainment	Transportation
Hobbies	Vacations

CHILDREN:

      Clothes   Medical

      Education   Toys

HOME-RELATED:

Appliances	Insurance
Electricity	Mortgage Payments
Food (eating out)	Property Taxes
Furnishings	Rent
Gas	Telephone
Groceries	Television, VCR, Etc.
Home Repairs	Trash Removal
House/Apt. Payments	Water

AUTOMOBILE:

Gas/Oil	Parking
Insurance	Payments
License	Repairs

This may seem like quite a task but remember, all these papers were not accumulated overnight. Also keep in mind that once this "paper monster" is processed into the system and put to rest, it will not have to be bothered with again, and the time and anxiety you will be spared later is well worth this effort now.

ITEM-DATE SORTING

Next, decide with what date you intend to begin your written record keeping. It is practical to start logging the documents that date from the first of the current year. This will save you much confusion later. However, if you want to take the time to do previous years, the same procedure applies. Here though, we will just be concerned with dates from January 1 of the present year.

Each item type is handled in the same way, so for an example we will use a home-related item - electricity. Take the stack of bills from your electric power company and sort them into years, as far back as they go. Put each year in a separate stack. Now take the current year aside. It doesn't matter if the present date is only a few weeks into the current year - just as long as you have at least one electric bill paid for this year.

Stack the other years neatly and separately and put a rubber band around each year's stack - then put these aside.

Now take the current year's electric bills and lay them out on the table surface so that they can be arranged in chronological order: (January, February, March, etc.) Stack them so the earliest date is on top and the rest proceed by month through the current year. Any bills that have not yet been paid, set aside from the others so they will not be mixed with the others and can receive your immediate attention.

If you are dealing with receipts, etc. that involve dates other than just monthly: First, separate them into their chronological months, beginning with January. Then take each month's stack and put it in "by-the-day" order: Jan. 3, Jan. 9, Jan. 15, Jan. 28, etc. Use this date-sorting procedure with all files for which you intend to keep running records.

How you handle your payments is up to you and we will not get into that here. This system is only concerned with making order out of paper chaos and getting your papers in order so that you can better see your position, thus making your own decisions easier.

Take two of the brown envelopes and with a black felt-tip pen, write "Electric Bills" on the front. Beneath this write the beginning and ending years for the stack of old bills. (Example: 1985 through 1987.) On the second envelope write "Electric Bills" on the front and below it write the current year (1988, 1989, etc.),

Put the packet of old electric bills in the first envelope and the current bills in the envelope marked with the current year.

Set them aside and do the same procedure with each of the items on your list, or the list above, whichever list you chose to use. Granted, this is somewhat of a tedious task but keep in mind that it is a one-time thing and you will not have to do it again, even for income taxes.

When sorting items such as clothing purchase receipts or grocery receipts that are not strictly on a monthly basis, an additional step in sorting is helpful and necessary. First, separate the slips into years. If you intend to keep the receipts for years past, bundle them up and put them in a brown envelope and mark it accordingly (with the item name and the beginning and ending years of the slips.

Take the slips for the current year and separate them into chronological months: January, February, March, etc. Now take each month stack and separate it into three piles: #1 pile: dates of that month from 1 to 10. #2 pile: dates of that months from 11 to 20, and #3 pile: dates from 21 through 31.

Finally, arrange each of these three stacks in proper daily chronological order so that the dates flow from the 1st through the 10th, the 11th through the 20th, and the 21st through the 31st. Stack these in the proper order (first #1, second #2, and third #3.

Do this with all non-monthly receipts, store them in the properly marked brown envelopes, and set them aside in one of the empty boxes.

KEEPING IMPORTANT DOCUMENTS

Documents like birth certificates, property deeds, automobile titles, marriage licenses, divorce decrees, insurance policies, etc. should be kept in a very safe place such as a bank safety deposit box. This would keep their loss by fire, theft or misplacement to a minimum. S.D. Boxes vary widely in price and size. For example: a box that measures 2" X 5" X 22" would rent for about $12.00 a year. A box 15" X 10" X 22" would rent for about $100.00 a year. The "average" practical size (4" x 10" X 22") would rent for about $35.00 a year. This is money well invested.

+-+-+-+-+-+-+-+-+-

Section 3. A Filing Plan

FILING

In order to get the Paper Monster in its cage, we use a familiar device known as filing. What follows is some background, examples, and a rundown of some basic rules.

Business and professional organizations of every type, large and small, have a need to store records for future reference. These records may include important facts about products, customers, employees, suppliers, and other necessary data. This information must be stored so that it remains safe, yet is quickly available for reference. This is achieved by using systematic filing procedures.

BUSINESS DEPENDS ON FILING

In business, filing is considered a part of "records management." It deals mostly with arrangement, classification and storage of records, in such a manner that, when needed, they may be quickly located.

In order to operate, every business man needs facts and figures, and properly set up files to get the right records to the right persons at the right time. Without such an arrangement, a business executive would not know for long what to do next and practically every type of business would shortly cease to operate.

EXAMPLE OF A BUSINESS FILING SYSTEM

The following example of a department store's credit sales system shows how dependent a typical business is on files. It shows the steps that are gone through, from the customer's applying for credit, until the first monthly bill is sent out.

STEPS

1. The customer files an application for credit.

2. The application is sent to the credit office where the customer's credit is checked out and found to be satisfactory.

3. The customer's application is put on file.

4. A charge card is sent to the customer by the credit department and this information is also added to the file.

5. The customer buys merchandise, using his charge card.

6. A two-copy sales slip is written up by the sales clerk and imprinted with the customer's charge card. One copy is given to the customer.

7. The other copy of the sales slip is sent to the accounts receivable department where it is posted to the customer's account.

8. The data on the sales slip is fed into the store's computer system under the customer's account name or number.

9. Any additional charge card purchases during the month by this customer are also fed (filed) into his computer account in this manner.

10. On the customer's monthly billing date his account is retrieved, a copy is printed out by the billing department and made ready to mail.

11. The bill is mailed to the customer.

SOME FILING BASICS

There are two basic methods of filing: filing by **name** and filing by **number.**

Probably the most common example of filing by name is the telephone directory. The basic requirement here is a knowledge of the alphabet in its natural sequence. When names are the important factor, such as in a doctor's office, this system is used.

A common example of the numeric filing system is that of house numbers. They usually begin in most cities at a central point and proceed outward along each street, zig-zagging from one side of the street to the other as the numbers increase.

The numeric system of filing is gaining more ground with the inroads of computer files and many cross-files are maintained by assigning a number to a client and cross referencing it with the client's name. Thusly, it is a simple matter to maintain and retrieve records of the same client under many different categories and quickly compile them into statistics. For instance: how many customers a company has in each state, how many are female, over 65, etc.

The numeric system is now used extensively in files maintained by government, credit card companies, banks, insurance companies, etc. The natural sequence of numbers make this a simple system to use, though much care in accuracy must be maintained; one wrong digit could cause havoc.

CAPTIONS

The name or number used to designate a file is called a caption. As an example: If you wish to keep a letter from the United Gas Company, then "United Gas Company" would be the name to use on the file, and all correspondence to and from the United Gas Company would be kept in this file.

Since the files we will be creating are basic, we will not have any numbered files.

MORE SCREENING

You have already sorted, saved and discarded many papers, as described in Section 2. At this point we will screen a little farther and decide which items are important enough to establish a file on them. Some things are a one-time item and it is pointless to clutter up a system with them. For example; a single old letter from a friend, or a paper you wrote in high school. It is best to file all such items under "Miscellany."

Use the sorting list in Section 2 as a guide to organizing and putting captions on your file folders. If you like to keep such things as mementos, make a file for those. But don't keep a lot of things you will never use or look at again. They have a way of expanding like fungi.

USING FILING CABINETS OR BOXES?

If you already have filing cabinets, so much the better. If not, two-drawer cabinets are inexpensive and available at most discount/department stores. These are worth the investment as, after all, you are setting up this system in order to keep and store your records in an orderly fashion and they deserve protection.

If you decide against using filing cabinets, cardboard boxes will do, except they make it a little more difficult to manipulate and they might get stored somewhere with other things and misplaced.

Use boxes that are wide enough to accommodate the file folders, and shallow enough to allow easy access to the filed materials. For greater ease in use, the folding parts of the top can be cut off or taped down to the sides.

PROTECTING YOUR RECORDS

A recent study of businesses that lost their records because of fire or other catastrophe showed that over 40 percent were not able to resume operation, because of this record loss.

Of course it is not suggested here that you rent a safety deposit box large enough for a filing cabinet (if they were available). But reasonable care should be taken in choosing a place for their storage. For instance, never store records on an unenclosed or unlocked porch or insecure area. After all, your records may not be worth much to someone else, but they are valuable to you and they are private.

USING THE FILE FOLDERS AND ENVELOPES

As you will notice, the file folders have a protruding tab at the top. This space is for writing the caption. Place the folded file folder on a table so that the tab is on the bottom sheet. This is the way they are to be used in the filing cabinets or boxes. With a medium-heavy black pen, print the caption on the tab so that it can be easily seen above the folder when it is in place in the file drawer or box. If, for example, this is a file for the water company, write "Water Company" on the tab. Now place this file folder in the file drawer (or box) with the caption (name) facing forward.

Take the brown envelope containing the water bills receipts and place them in this folder. If you have envelopes containing the old and a new bills and receipts, place them both in this file. In fact, anything relating to the Water Company - any communications or business with them, keep this also in this file so you will know where it all is and can quickly find it should the need arise.

Now take another subject - let's say insurance. Take another file folder and using the same procedure as before, write on the tab "Insurance." Place this in the file drawer or box <u>in front of</u> "Water", since "I" comes before "W" in the alphabet. Now place the envelopes marked "Insurance" in this file.

Continue doing this with all of the subjects you have designated until they are all filed away. Make sure they are filed in alphabetical order so they can be found easily.

In the next chapter we will take up the correct method of filing that will make finding your papers much easier. But already you have made great strides in conquering the paper monster - so let's continue.

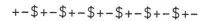

A file folder.

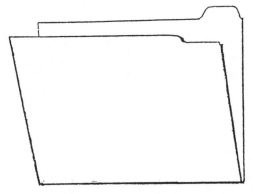

CUT SINGLE

CUT HALVES

CUT THIRDS

CUT FOURTHS

File folders may be had in
various colors and tab widths.

CUT FIFTHS

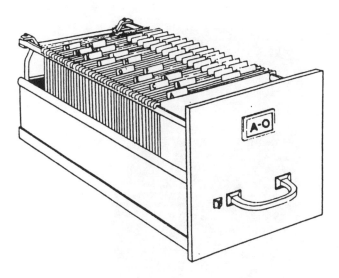

File drawer with hanging
file folders.

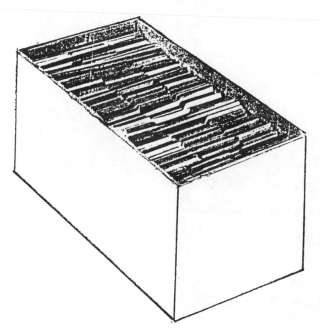

Box with file folders and files.

Two-drawer file cabinet.

Four-drawer file cabinet
with drop front drawers.

Section 4. How To File

In order to use the basic system of this book it is not essential that you are familiar with professional filing techniques. However, the information presented in this chapter will be of great help - and this is valuable general knowledge. Following are some standard basic rules that take the mystery out of correct filing.

INDEXING

As you learned in the previous chapter, caption names identify records in files. These captions may be either words or numbers, for our purposes however, we will be dealing only with words. This section will lay out the correct rules for alphabetic filing. This procedure is known as indexing.

As an example: if you index the name Glenn Mullins, you would use the same procedure as that employed by the telephone directories and index by last names. Therefore, you would look under M, not G. So the correct indexing for Glenn Mullins would be Mullins, Glenn.

If each person decided to file by his own rules it would be very difficult or impossible for another person to locate records in the files. Therefore, standard rules must be used by everyone doing the filing or no one else, and maybe not even the person filing, could later retrieve the information they are looking for.

TERMS FOR INDEXING

The parts of a file name are called <u>units</u>. Example: Charles F. Gates would have three units. Transposed to the proper filing order they would read: Gates, Charles F. Unit #1 is the last name, Gates; Unit #2 is the first name, Charles; and Unit #3 is the middle initial, F.

The term <u>alphabetizing</u> is used to indicate the files in the system are organized according to the natural sequence of the letters of the alphabet. A, B, C, D, etc. If the first letter of last names are the same, then the second letter is considered. If that is the same, then the third letter, and so on.

The following is a list of person's names in random order, then the same names listed in their proper filing order.

NAMES IN THEIR NATURAL ORDER

Arthur Harold

Vivian L. Tetlock

William T. Gosmond

Simon F. McSnade

Simon D. McSnade

Mortomer Reudstead

Fred Velecke

THE SAME NAMES TRANSPOSED FOR FILING AND ALPHABETIZED

<u>Unit 1.   Unit 2. Unit 3.</u>

Gosmond, William T.

Harold, Arthur

McSnade, Simon   D.

McSnade, Simon   F.

Tetlock, Vivian L.

You will notice that each name in the second list is in alphabetical sequence, also Simon F. McSnade is filed <u>after</u> Simon D. McSnade, since F occurs after D in the alphabet.

MORE NAMES

Fred Yates

James Donald Cook

James Cook

Fredrick V. Yates

THE SAME NAMES TRANSPOSED FOR FILING AND ALPHABETIZED

Cook, James

Cook, James Donald

Farmer, Felix A.

Farmer, Felix J.

Yates, Fred

Yates, Fredrick V.

The Rules For Filing

RULE 1. NAMES OF INDIVIDUALS

Alphabetize and transpose the names of individuals in this order: Surname or last name first, given name or first name (or initial) second, and middle name or initial, if any, third.

NAME	PROPER INDEXING ORDER
Joan Marie Adams	Adams, Joan Marie
Tom J. Baker	Baker, Tom J.
J. Edgar Swint	Swint, J. Edgar
Beasley B. Wayne	Wayne, Beaseley B.

RULE 2. IN ALPHABETIC ORDER

Alphabetize the names by comparing the first unit in each name, letter by letter. Only consider the second units when the first units are identical. If the first and second units are identical, then only is the third unit considered, and so on.

NAME:	UNIT 1	UNIT 2	UNIT 3
Resemary L. Williams	Williams,	Rosemary	L.
Rosenary M. Williams	Williams,	Resemary	M.
Ann Wright	Wright,	Ann.	
Annie Wright	Wright,	Annie	

RULE 3. THE SURNAME ALONE OR WITH INITIAL

When a surname is used alone, it is listed the same surname with a first name or initial. A surname with only a first initial is listed before the same surname beginning with the same letters as the initial. This rule is sometimes referred to as, "Nothing comes before something."

NAME:	UNIT 1	UNIT 2	UNIT 3
Snediker	Snediker		
E. Snediker	Snediker,	E.	
Ely Snediker	Snediker,	Ely	
Thompson	Thompson		
F. Thompson	Thompson,	F.	
Frank J. Thompson	Thompson,	Frank	J.

RULE 4. PREFIXES TO SURNAMES

A prefix, in this case, is an attachment to the beginning of a name.

A prefix to a surname is not a separate indexing unit but is considered part of the surname. Prefixes include: d', D', Da, De, De, Del, Des, Di, Du, Fitz, La, Le, M', Mac, Mc, O', St., Van, Van der, Von, Von der, etc. M', Mac, and Mc prefixes are indexed exactly as they are spelled. The prefix St. (the abbreviation for saint) is indexed as though the word Saint was spelled out.

NAME:	UNIT 1	UNIT 2	UNIT 3
John DeForest	DeForest,	John	
Ruth C. LaChien	LaChien,	Ruth	C.
Ray MacDonald	MacDonald,	Ray	
William R. St. Denis	Saint Denis	William	R.
Helen May Van Doren	Van Doren,	Helen	May

RULE 5. COMPANY OR FIRM NAMES

Unless it contains the name of an individual, the units in a company or firm, or institution name are used in the same sequence as normally written. Also, if a foreign word happens to be the first word, it is considered part of the word that follows it, and not a separate indexing unit.

NAME:	UNIT 1	UNIT 2	UNIT 3
Beane Lumber Company	Beane	Lumber	Company
Diane's Diner	Diane's	Diner	
Loew's Locks, Inc.	Loew's	Locks	Inc
Murphy Liquor Dlivery	Murphy	Liquor	Delivery

RULE 6. COMPLETE INDIVIDUAL NAMES WITHIN FIRM NAMES

If the institution, company or firm name includes the complete name of an individual, the units in the individual's name are transposed, (as when dealing with individual names only).

NAME:I	UNIT 1	UNIT 2	UNIT 3	UNIT 4
Don A. Bass Jewelers	Bass,	Don	A.	Jewelers
Bradford Box Company	Bradford	Box	Company	
A. L. Trent Inc.	Trent,	A.	L.	Inc.
B. Dillon Architect	Dillon,	B.	Architect	

RULE 7. ABBREVIATIONS

Index abbreviations as though the words represented were written out in full. Single letters that are <u>not</u> abbreviations are treated as separate indexing units.

NAME:I	UNIT 1	UNIT 2	UNIT 3	UNIT 4
ABC Cafe	A	B	C	Cafe
Central Sta. Cab Co.	Central	Station	Cab	Company
Chas. Evans Clothes	Evans,	Charles	Clothes	
Gates News Serv.	Gates	News	Service	
Hill St. Bakery	Hill	Street	Bakery	
Wm. Wyler Plumbers	Wyler,	William	Plumbers	

RULE 8. THE ARTICLE "THE"

In indexing,"The" is not considered a unit and is therefore disregarded.

In regard to labeling file folders, when a "the" occurs at the beginning of a name, it is placed in parentheses at the end. Should "the" occur in the middle of a name, place it in parentheses but do not move it.

NAME:I	UNIT 1	UNIT 2	UNIT 3	UNIT 4
Jobob The Printer	Jobob	Printer		
The First State Bank	First	State	Bank	
The J. K. Hines Co.	Hines,	J.	K.	Company
The Red Herring	Red	Herring		

RULE 9. NAMES THAT ARE HYPHENATED

A hyphen between words in a firm name causes them to be treated as separate units. If the surname of an individual is hyphenated, the complete surname is treated as one indexing unit. This also applies to the hyphenated names of individuals when the complete name is part of a firm name.

NAME:	UNIT 1	UNIT 2	UNIT 3	UNIT 4
May-Day Flower Co.	May-	Day	Flower	Company
One-Shot Auto Repair	One-	Shot	Auto	Repair
Trevor-Robins Shirts	Trevor-Robins	Shirts		
One-On-One Brick Co.	One-On-One	Brick	Company	
A-1 Glue Co.	A-	1	Glue	Company

RULE 10. PREPOSITIONS, CONJUNCTIONS, AND COMPANY NAME ENDINGS

Prepositions and conjunctions such as: for, as, &, in, of, are not usually considered as units in indexing but are included if they are part of a firm name. Firm endings such as Bros., Co., Corp., Inc., Ltd., Mfg., and Son, are used as indexing units.

The above prepositions and conjunctions are written on filing cards and folders in their normal sequence.

NAME:I	UNIT 1	UNIT 2	UNIT 3	UNIT 4
H and R Root Tea	H and	R	Root	Tea
J & R Express Co.	J &	R	Express	Company
Full-of-Life Herbs	Full-of	Life	Herbs	
Wendell & Son Mfg.	Wendell &	Son	Manufacturing	

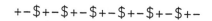

+-$+-$+-$+-$+-$+-$+-

Section 5. Setting Up Your Filing System

Now that you have all the necessary ingredients, it is now time to put them all together into an efficient filing system in which you can easily store and retrieve your papers, old and new.

PUTTING IT ALL TOGETHER

Place the filing cabinet where you intend to keep it permanently. Take out one of the drawers and place it on the work surface. If you are using a box instead, do the same with that.

If you have not marked the file folders yet, shuffle them so that the tabs are staggered for easier reading when in the box or file drawer. Use a medium point, black felt tip pen and mark the names of the categories (captions) on the tabs of the file folders. Below is a reminder list:

REMINDER LIST

PERSONAL:

Clothes	Investments
Contributions	Medical, Dental, Etc.
Credit Cards	Memberships
Education	Taxes
Entertainment	Transportation
Hobbies	Vacations
Insurance	

CHILDREN:

| Clothes | Medical |
| Education | Toys |

HOME-RELATED:

Appliances*	Insurance
Electricity	Mortgage Payments
Food (eating out)	Property Taxes
Furnishings	Rent
Gas	Telephone
Groceries	Television, VCR, Etc.
Home Repairs	Trash Removal
House/Apt. Payments	Water

AUTOMOBILE:

Gas/Oil	Parking
Insurance	Payments
License	Repairs

Next, put the file folders in the file drawer or box in alphabetical order, starting with the "Appliance" folder. Put these in the front of the drawer or box and work on toward the back and through the alphabet.

When all the labeled file folders are in the drawer or box, take the envelopes and packets of papers and match the names on these with the names on the file folders and put each envelope and packet in its proper place.

Great! You now have your paper monster safe in his cage. Hang in there - there is only a little more to do.

Put the file drawer back in its cabinet, or the box in its storing place. We will get back to their contents a little later.

APPLIANCE MANUALS

Who among us has not misplaced, lost, or thrown out the instruction manual, warranty, and manufacturer's address that came with a radio, VCR, telephone - or even a refrigerator, piano or a new car? This can be a frustrating situation when something goes wrong, or a new feature is discovered and getting it to work is a mystery. Make good use of your "Appliance" and "Automobile" files for this purpose.

PURGING THE FILES

From time to time, especially if the filing cabinets or boxes get crowded, it is a good practice to thin out or "purge" your files. If the documents are already logged in the ledgers, the papers are over several years old and are not of a legal nature (such as a deed, etc.), or if is no longer important or necessary, take it out of the files and throw them away. Before you discard these papers however, lay them aside for a few days and let your unconscious mind decide if there is a need to keep them. If you get no positive message, then out they go. This purging can be done at regular intervals, like every six months or once a year.

+-$+-$+-$+-$+-$+-

Section 6. Checking Accounts and Check Registers

Your checkbook is your <u>main business record</u> and should be kept up-to-date at all times. It should tell you at a glance: how much money you have in your account, what checks you have written, plus: when, to whom, and for how much.

The familiar phrase "I can't balance my checkbook." is a a common expression heard throughout the land. This chapter offers some suggestions for keeping the problem to a minimum.

A strong inducement to keeping one's checkbook up to date and in balance is the fees banks charge for overdrafts. Depending on the bank, these charges range from $10.00 to $20.00 per item and some banks invoke this charge for a returned check, regardless of the reason it was returned.

SOME BANKING DEFINITIONS

bank draft: A check drawn by a bank on another bank, payable to a third party.

check: A draft on a bank drawn against deposited funds to pay a specified sum of money to a specified person or organization on demand.

overdraw: To draw checks on a bank account for more than the balance.

stop payment: A depositor's order to a bank to refuse to honor a specified check drawn by the depositor.

IDENTIFYING ACCOUNTS

There are several systems used by banks and the federal government for identifying checking accounts. One such subscription service is known as CHEX System. All checking accounts must bear the Social Security number of their owner. By using this number, all checking accounts in the United States can be almost instantly identified, no matter in what names they were opened.

DIFFERENCES IN CHECK REGISTERS

The blank form for entering check information is called the check register. Probably the widest used type is the so-called "pocket" register. This small book of blank forms, along with a pad of checks and deposit slips is provided in a small plastic folder, issued with your purchase of checks when you open a checking account at a bank.

These are compact and convenient but there is often some ambiguity among the register form inserts, since there is no really standard format. Note the differences in the column headings on the following page of pocket registers: From form A to B, the columns for the check number and date have been transposed. Also reversed are the debit and credit columns. Should you be supplied form A to replace form B (or vica-versa) and not notice the difference, problems could easily arise.

POCKET REGISTER A.

		RECORD ALL CHARGES OR CREDITS THAT AFFECT YOUR ACCOUNT					
NUMBER	DATE	DESCRIPTION OF TRANSACTION	PAYMENT/DEBIT (-)	√ T	FEE (IF ANY) (-)	DEPOSIT/CREDIT (+)	BALANCE $
			$		$	$	

POCKET REGISTER B.

19_____ BE SURE TO DEDUCT ANY PER ITEM CHARGES, SERVICE CHARGES, OR FEES THAT MAY APPLY.

DATE	NUMBER	TRANSACTION DESCRIPTION	(+ OR −) OTHER	√ T	(+) AMOUNT OF DEPOSIT	(−) AMOUNT OF PAYMENT OR WITHDRAWAL	BALANCE

OTHER TYPES OF CHECK REGISTERS

There is also the "desk" type of check register used by some small businesses. These have three or more checks to a page and the record of transaction is kept on the check stub, which remains in the checkbook when the check is removed.

A desk register that has much practical utility can be had by using a 3 or 4 column ledger book. (Ledger books and their use will be taken up in detail in the next section.) Below is a reproduction of a page from such a check register:

YEAR DATE	CK.#	DESCRIPTION	PAYMENT (1)	DEPOSIT CREDIT (2)	BALANCE (3)
					$ 555.25
1-6	223	JOHN'S GROCERY	36.00		36.00
					519.25

REFINEMENTS TO THE LEDGER-TYPE CHECK REGISTER

Inside the front or back cover of your ledger check register, make a pocket of a small envelope and affix it with transparent tape. This will serve as a storage place for your current book of checks.

Carrying a checkbook with you is a little risky. Should you lose it, you would have to close your account. An alternative would be to carry two or three checks in your billfold and record their numbers on a card, (which you keep in the pocket of the check ledger with the book of checks). If you lose the carried checks, simply call the bank and issue a "stop payment order" for the lost check numbers. (There will be a charge.) When you use one of the carried checks, make a note of the details and check number and later enter them in the check ledger, then cross off that number on the card.

BALANCING YOUR CHECKBOOK

Balancing or reconciling your checking account is not the formidable task it sometimes appears to be. Of course, if it has been in disarray for a long time, the task of bringing it in balance will be more difficult. On occasion it may be better to accept the bank's figure for your account balance and start anew from that point, rather than tracking your account, check by check, for months or years.

Following is one method for getting your checking account back on the track:

Checking Account Reconciliation

Checks Outstanding

DATE/ CHECK #	DOLLARS	CENTS
TOTAL		

A

1. Ending balance shown on your most recent statement. $........

2. Total deposits not shown on statement. $........

3. Add lines 1 and 2. $........

4. Enter total of checks outstanding from line A at left. $........

5. Subtract line 4 from line 3. $........

6. Enter any payments or withdrawals not shown on statement. $........

7. Subtract line 6 from line 5.   TOTAL B $........

8. Enter balance from your check register. $........

9. Enter total of any service charges, etc. $........

10. Subtract line 9 from line 8. $........

11. Enter any earnings to this account. $........

12. Add lines 10 and 11.   TOTAL C $........

TOTAL C should equal TOTAL B.

+-$+-$+-$+-$+-$+-$+-

Section 7. Ledger Books

The ledger book is the final ingredient in, and the heart of our system. It enables us to have a great deal of information from many sources in one place and easily accessible. According to Random House dictionary, a ledger is "an account book of final entry containing all the accounts."

There are several kinds of ledger books and sheets: the regular bound ledger book, the post bound ledger book (a sort of semi-permanent bound loose leaf book used by large companies and organizations), and ledger sheets in pads. All of these are available in various sizes, the average sizes ranging from 7 1/2" X 9 1/2" to 8 12/" X 11".

Ledger pages are ruled into lines and columns, also in various sizes and number of column rulings. Books and columnar pads are available in single page with 2, 3, 4, 5 and 6 column and with 8, 10, 12 and 14 column in double-page format.

WHAT YOU WILL NEED

One or more ledger books, bound or padded. The bound books are more durable and there is a rather wide price range.

Two fine-point felt tip pens, one black ink and one red ink - for making neat entries and dividers in the ledgers.

A small calculator. It is good to be able to do your own figuring but a calculator is more foolproof.

A 12-inch ruler for making straight lines.

A bottle of correction fluid, such as Liquid Paper or White Out. Get the type used for covering pen writing, (not for typewriter or copy machine). This is also available in shades to match the color of the pages in the ledgers.

A small packet of self-stick labels approx. 1 1/2" X 3". These are for labeling the ledger books.

WHERE TO FIND THESE ITEMS

Except for the ledger books or pads, all of these items should be easily available at office/school supply sections of any department/discount or drug store. The ledger books may be obtained from office supply stores. Just in case you have difficulty locating the kind of ledger books you desire, following are the addresses of some manufacturers:

MANUFACTURERS OF LEDGER BOOKS & PADS

"Multi-Column book"
Wilson Jones Company, 6150 Toughy Ave.
Chicago, IL 60648

"Columnar Book"
Boorum & Pease Company, 801-T Newark Ave.
Elizabeth, NJ 07208

Borum & Pease also manufactures "Accountant Work Sheet

Pad", a soft cover columned book available in 2 to 12 col. 8 1/2 X 11". Ans: National Brand "Analysis Pad" by Dennison National Company, Sullivan Road (P.O.Box 791), Holyoke, MA 01041

USING THE LEDGER BOOKS

You can get by with using just one ledger book, but if you prefer to keep your personal finances separate from the home, etc., then two books would be better. Also, if you have any kind of small enterprise or business going, you most certainly would want to have a separate ledger book for that. And the use of another ledger book for a check register is very practical. Unless you intend to purchase large "professional" ledgers, considering the time they will last, the cost factor is insignificant.

Some of the better ledger books have consecutively numbered pages and line numbers. This is for easy location of an item and legal and auditing purposes.

SETTING UP THE COLUMNS

One ledger book can accommodate several groups of multi-column subjects. Be sure to allow enough pages for each group. For example, allow enough space for each double-page column group to accommodate, for example, five years of entries. If we are thinking of insurance payments for an average household, five double pages should be sufficient for this record period.

SUGGESTIONS FOR GROUPINGS

Here are some suggestions for grouping your subjects. Each overall group is called a <u>category</u>: (Individual, Home-Related, Children, Automobile. Next is the <u>unit</u>: Financial, Health, Personal, Insurance, etc. These column heading suggested lists are used as a guideline which you may use or delete as you see fit.

SUGGESTED COLUMNS

INDIVIDUAL-

UNIT 1. FINANCIAL	UNIT 2. HEALTH
Contributions	Medical
Credit Card Fees	Dental
Taxes	Fitness

UNIT 3. PERSONAL	UNIT 4. INSURANCE
Clothes	Health
Entertainment	Life
Hobbies	Other
Vacations	

UNIT 5. SELF-IMPROVEMENT

Books	Memberships
Education	Videos

HOME-RELATED-

UNIT 1. FINANCIAL	UNIT 2. UTILITIES
Home Insurance	Electricity
Home Repairs	Gas
Mortgage Payments	Telephone
Property Taxes	Trash Removal
Rent	Water

UNIT 3. FURNISHINGS	UNIT 4. FOOD
Appliances	Groceries
Furniture	Eating Out
TV, VCR, Etc.	Entertainment

CHILDREN-

UNIT 1. ORDINARY	UNIT 2. EXTRAORDINARY
Clothes	Books
Insurance	Music
Medical	Sports
School	Toys

AUTOMOBILE-

UNIT 1. FINANCIAL	UNIT 2. USE
Insurance	Gas/Oil
Monthly Payments	Parking
License	Repair

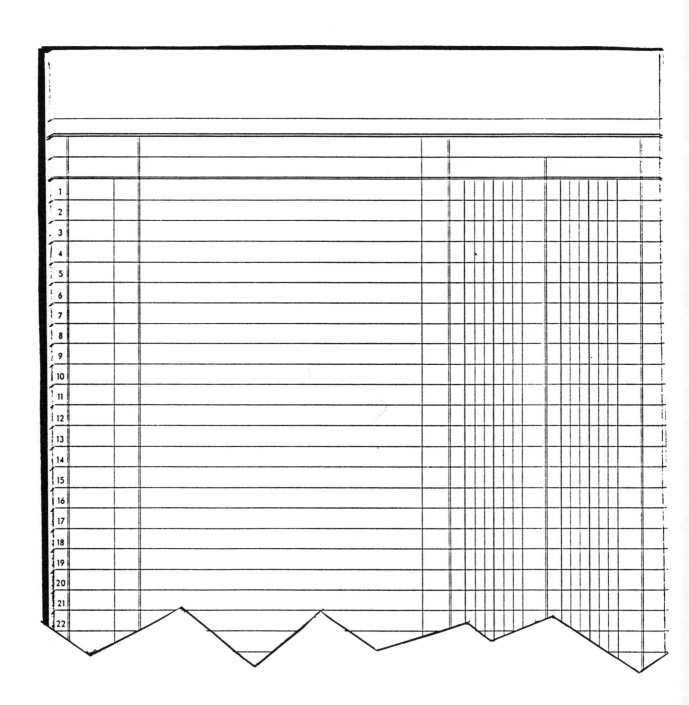

A two-column ledger page.

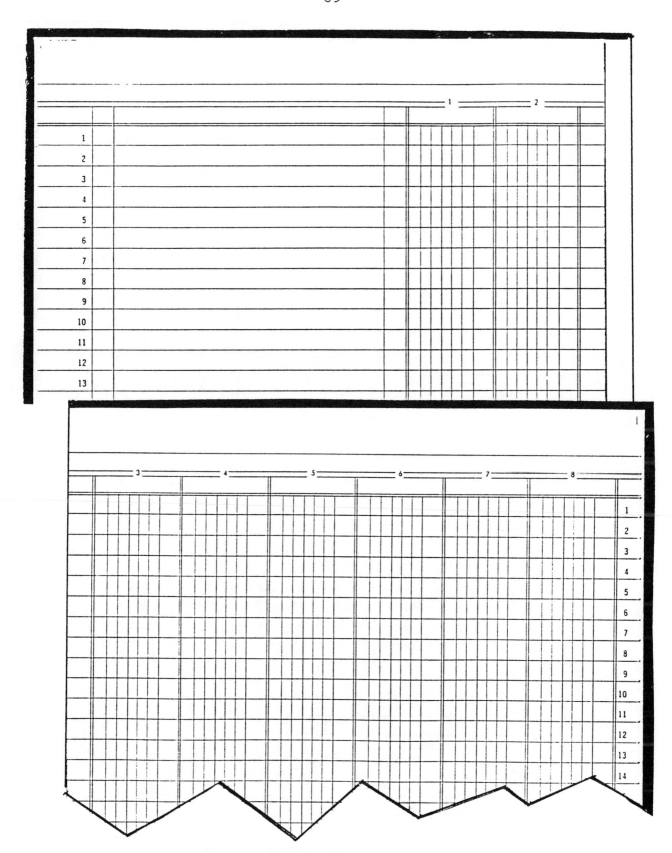

Eight-column ledger pages (Read across both pages)

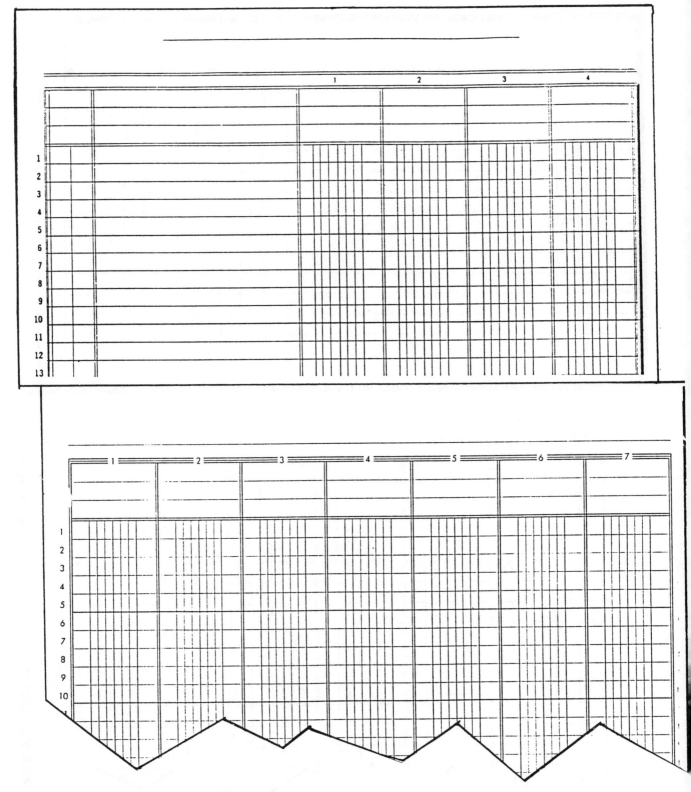

Eleven-column ledger pages (read across)

+-$+-$+-$+-$+-$+-$+-$+-

Section 8. Entering Your Files In The Ledgers

We are now ready for the final operation in this organizing system - setting up the ledgers and entering the information. When you complete this section, all the information you will probably ever need from your former mounds of paper will be in these few ledger books, ready for instant retrieval - and without the use of a computer.

At this point you may logically ask, "If the information on the papers is going to be in the ledgers, why keep the original papers?" The answer is: should you be required for some reason to produce the original paid bill, receipt, etc., at some later date for proof of the transaction, it should be kept in the files for a "reasonable" period of time.

DIVIDING UP THE PAGES

Take a ledger book that has 6 or 8 columns and, if the pages are not numbered or the page count is not indicated inside the front cover, count the pages. This could vary from 36 to 80, depending on the book. Also, when dealing with over six columns, they are usually in a double page format: that is, they read across both pages.

Do not use the first (right side) page of a ledger book unless you are using a one-page format. Begin all double-page formats on the left page so thay can be read straight across.

Allow each unit or group of items about 5 double pages. Put a slip of paper between the pages at each group division you have counted off and be sure there is enough room in the book for all the 5 double-page groups you will need for a complete category of groups. If the book is too small for this, get a book with more pages.

Tabs for the pages where each category section begins may be purchased or made from colored plastic tape. Select a color and cut several lengths about two inches long. At the top of the left hand pages where you have placed the paper markers, select a spot about 2 inches from the left corner of the page. With the tape extending up from the top of the page, carefully press 1/2 inch of the tape to the paper. Fold the tape over in the center, bringing it back down and press another 1/2 inch to the back of this page. You now have a 1/2 inch tab of red, green, or whatever, extending up 1/2 inch for ease in finding and opening the ledger book at these section beginnings.

WRITING IN THE LEDGER SPACES

Ledger books are designed primarily for bookkeeping style entries and thus are produced with fine lines and "tiny" spaces for the orderly entering of columns of neat figures. For our purposes, however, such meticulous entries are not necessary. Do try to be reasonably neat and keep the numbers in their proper columns and lines. As long as they are clearly legible and do not cause confusion, your entry is fine.

PUTTING IN THE COLUMN HEADINGS

We will use one of the ledger books and enter some of the subject units in it to give you the feel of the operation. You can use this as a guide for similar entries. Again, be sure to allow enough pages between categories and units to accommodate the addition of entries you anticipate over a period of time. The 5 double-pages you have counted off should be adequate for a year of most items. If you feel a certain subject needs more room, allow more pages.

Do not write the column headings in longhand - unless your handwriting is exceptionally neat and legible. Use the black ink pen and print neatly, being sure to keep the printing in the prescribed space provided. Sloppy headings and entries that are not neat and difficult to read are a nuisance to behold, and also may cause problems later when totalling the columns or gathering information from the ledgers for a specific purpose. If information is not correct, sometimes it is worse than none. Be neat - it pays.

Let's begin with the first category, INDIVIDUAL. Open the book and turn to the first page so you are at the first double page. Begin entering the headings you will use. As you can see, each item has its own column and only figures relating to that particular item should go into that column. For these examples we will use the column names in the lists. If you make mistakes, use the correction fluid.

(Size Reduced)

INDIVIDUAL
FINANCIAL

	YEAR -DATE	PAID TO:	CONTRI- BUTIONS	CREDIT CARD FEES	TAXES	OTHER
1						
2						
3						
4						
5						
6						

INDIVIDUAL
HEALTH

	YEAR -DATE	PAID TO:	MEDICAL	DENTAL	FITNESS	OTHER
1						
2						
3						
4						
5						
6						

INDIVIDUAL
PERSONAL

	YEAR -DATE	PAID TO:	CLOTHES	ENTER- TAINMENT	HOBBIES	VACATIONS
1						
2						
3						
4						
5						
6						
7						
8						

INDIVIDUAL

SELF-IMPROVEMENT

YEAR -DATE	PAID TO:	BOOKS	EDUCATION	MEMBER- SHIPS	VIDEOS
1					
2					
3					
4					
5					
6					

HOME-RELATED

FINANCIAL

YEAR -DATE	PAID-TO	HOME INSURANCE	HOME REPAIRS	MORTGAGE PAYMENTS	RENT-OR PROPERTY TAXES
1					
2					
3					
4					
5					
6					

HOME-RELATED

UTILITIES

YEAR -DATE	PAID TO:	ELECT-RICITY	GAS	WATER	TELE-PHONE
1					
2					
3					
4					
5					
6					
7					
8					

HOME-RELATED
FURNISHINGS

YEAR DATE	PAID-TO:	APPLIANCES	FURNITURE	TV, VCR	OTHER
1					
2					
3					
4					
5					
6					

HOME-RELATED
FOOD

YEAR DATE	PAID TO:	GROCERIES	EATING OUT	ENTERTAINING	OTHER
1					
2					
3					
4					
5					
6					

CHILDREN
ORDINARY

YEAR DATE	PAID TO:	CLOTHES	INSURANCE	MEDICAL	SCHOOL
1					
2					
3					
4					
5					
6					
7					
8					

CHILDREN
EXTRAORDINARY

		1	2	3	4
YEAR -DATE	PAID TO:	BOOKS	MUSIC	SPORTS	TOYS
1					
2					
3					
4					
5					
6					

AUTOMOBILE
FINANCIAL

		1	2	3	4
YEAR -DATE	PAID TO:	INSURANCE	MONTHLY PAYMENTS	LICENSE	OTHER
1					
2					
3					
4					
5					
6					

AUTOMOBILE
USE

		1	2	3	4
YEAR -DATE	PAID TO:	GASOLINE & OIL	PARKING	REPAIR	OTHER
1					
2					
3					
4					
5					
6					
7					
8					

MISCELLANEOUS
HOME SHOP

YEAR-DATE	PAID TO:	HAND TOOLS	POWER TOOLS	ELEC-TRICAL	OTHER	
1						1
2						2
3						3
4						4
5						5
6						6

MISCELLANEOUS
YARD

YEAR-DATE	PAID TO:	PAID GARDENING	SUPPLIES	YARD EQUIPMENT	OTHER	
1						1
2						2
3						3
4						4
5						5
6						6

MISCELLANEOUS
RVS AND UPKEEP

YEAR-DATE	PAID TO:	BICYCLES	BOAT	MOTOR-CYCLE	OTHER	
1						1
2						2
3						3
4						4
5						5
6						6
7						7
8						8

MAKING SOME ENTRIES

From your file drawer or box, take out your insurance receipts and records for the current year. Separate them by type (life, health, etc.), then separate these by the issuing companies. Take each company stack and put it in chronological order, beginning with January 1 of the current year. This can be done more easily by first separating it into months, then dates in the month.

Since most persons and families have insurance with several companies, it is a good idea to use the name of the insurance companies as column headings. A notation of whether it is for a life or a health policy, or whatever, should be included in parentheses near the company name.

INSURANCE DUE DATES

Use one of the columns for "Next Date Due", usually the column on the far right, allowing some blank columns in between in case you add new policies. You might consider using red or orange ink for this column heading - and also for making the entries of the next due date, each time you make a payment on a policy. This will help to remind you of the importance of this column.

Once this insurance record system is set up and kept up to date, it is then only necessary to open your ledger book at the insurance section and see at a glance when the next payment is due for any policy you have.

INDIVIDUAL
INSURANCE

			1	2	3	4
1987 DATE PAID	REMARKS		PERIOD PAID	NEXT DATE -DUE-	POLICY BEGAN	POLICY DROPPED
1	1-18	PAYS ON HOSPITAL ROOM	1 YEAR	1-18-88	1-18-87	
2	2-4		1 MO.	3-1-87		
3	2-18		3 MO.	6-1-87		
4	3-8		1 MO.	4-15-87		
5	3-9	LIFE + DISMEMB.	1 YR.	6-20-88		
6	"		6 MO.	9-1-87		
7	4-1		6 MO.	11-1-87		
8	"		3 MO.	7-15-87		
9	5-15		3 MO.	9-1-87		
10						
11						
12						

INDIVIDUAL
MEDICAL

			1	2	3	4
YEAR DATE PAID	PAID TO= REMARKS		MEDICAL	DENTAL	OPTICAL	HOSPITAL
1	1-3	DR. LUKE (2 RESTORATIVES)		44.00		
2	3-20	" (CLEANING)		25.00		
3	3-29	AID-RITE DRUG STORE				
4	4-15	DR. DOORIGHT (OFFICE-VISIT)	21.00			
5	5-20	DR SQUINT (EYES EXAM.)			30.00	
6	5-30	PARALAX OPTICAL Co.(GLASSES)			120.00	
7	6-10	DR. DOORIGHT (CHECKUP)	75.00			
8	6-11	AID-RITE DRUG STORE				
9						
10						
11						
12						
13						
14						
15						

(Read across both pages.)

PRUDEN-TIAL HOSPITAL	PRUDEN-TIAL LIFE	OLD AMER. ACCIDENT	SENTRY MAJ. MED.	PHYSICIANS MUTUAL HOSPITAL	AARP HOSPITAL	
				204.60		
	18.60					
33.43						
					18.80	
		31.00				
	111.60					
			126.00			
					56.40	
33.43						

RX	MEDICINE	RX#	DR.	FOR:		
5.25	LENOXIN	2127590	DOORIGHT	HEART		
14.50	DESYREL	2128622	DOORIGHT	HORMONES		

INDIVIDUAL
PERSONAL

	YEAR-DATE PAID	PAID TO:	CLOTHES	ENTER-TAINMENT	HOBBIES	VACATIONS
			1	2	3	4
1	1-15	DOWDY BROS. (SUIT)	220.00			
2	1-30	AJAX VIDEO		30.00		
3	"	MOVIE		5.00		
4	2-10	F&M HOBBY SHOP (TRAIN)			125.00	
5	2-14	" " accessories			36.00	
6	3-2	2 weeks in FLORIDA				1,130.00
7	4-1	DOWDY BROS. (SHIRTS)	96.00			
8	4-15	AJAX VIDEO		25.00		
9	5-6	STAMP PALACE			46.00	
10	5-8	MOVIE (FOR 2)		10.00		
11	5-18	DOWDY BROS (SHOES)	85.00			
12	"	" " " (spt. coat)	165.00			
13	6-1	MYSTERY VIDEO		29.00		
14	"	WESTERN CLASSICS		45.00		
15	6-15	TRIP TO CANADA				955.00
16	6-29	MOVIE (2)		10.00		
17	7-2	K-MART (SOCKS)	18.00			
18	7-3	DOWDY BROS. (RAINCOAT)	130.00			
19	7-4	STAMP WORLD			22.00	
20	7-8	TRIP TO DALLAS				1,200.00
21	8-5	STAMP WORLD			31.00	
22	8-6	MOVIE (2)		10.00		
23	8-8	K-MART (HANDKERCHIEFS)	15.00			
24	8-10	MYSTERY VIDEO		35.00		
25	8-14	DOWDY BROS (PANTS)	55.00			

(Size Reduced)

INDIVIDUAL
SELF-IMPROVEMENT

#	YEAR-DATE PAID	PAID TO:	Books	Education	Member- ships	Videos
1	1-6	MAJOR'S BOOK STORE	19.95			
2	1-8	SMITHERS UNIV. (TUITION)		310.00		
3	"	TEXT BOOKS	85.00			
4	"	SUPPLIES		61.00		
5	1-25	BOOK OF MONTH CLUB			15.00	
6	2-5	PCB	24.50			
7	2-8	BARNES & NOBLE	18.75			
8	3-1	STUDY VIDEOS				49.95
9	3-16	RAPID READING INST.			39.00	
10	4-2	MAJOR'S BOOK STORE	25.00			
11	4-18	HISTORIC VIDEOS				41.00
12	5-7	PCB	18.00			
13	6-4	STUDY VIDEOS				49.95
14	6-6	SMITHERS UNIV. (SUMMER)		120.00		
15	6-7	TEXT BOOKS	40.00			
16	"	SUPPLIES		24.00		
17	"	SUB. TO READER'S FORUM			24.00	
18	7-4	MOORE'S BOOKS	19.95			
19	7-14	COSMIC VIDEOS				35.00
20	7-30	SMITHERS UNIV. (FALL)		310.00		
21	8-6	BARNES & NOBLE	24.00			
22	"	SIMON & SCHUSTER	16.50			
23	8-14	THINK BIG CLUB			30.00	
24	8-18	PASE VIDEOS				27.50
25	9-1	MOORE'S BOOKS	5.50			
26						
27						
28						
29						
30						
31						
32						
33						
34						

HOME-RELATED
FURNISHINGS

#	YEAR DATE PAID	PAID-TO:	1 APPLIANCES	2 FURNITURE	3 TV, VCR	4 OTHER
1	1-15	SEARS (EASY CHAIR)		300.00		
2	"	" (WASHER)	350.00			
3	2-5	DELMAR DEPT. STORE (VACUUM CLEANER)				150.00
4	2-6	K-MART (SPACE HEATER)				25.00
5	3-12	SEARS (VCR)			345.00	
6	3-30	LOEW'S (UTILITY STAND)				50.00
7	4-10	WARD'S (MICROWAVE OVEN)	135.00			
8	4-12	MARTY'S (LAMP)				41.00
9	4-30	" (ROLL TOP DESK)		230.00		
10	5-1	LOEW'S (BAR STOOLS)		95.00		
11	5-25	" (LAWN FURNITURE)		125.00		
12	6-2	SEARS (SMALL TV)			310.00	
13	6-6	MARTY'S (CARPET)				395.00
14	"	" (CHAIR)		35.00		
15	"	" (PICTURE)				35.00
16	"	" (VASE)				10.00
17	7-4	PENNEY'S (RANGE)	399.00			
18	"	" (TOWELS)				29.00
19	"	" (BATH MAT)				15.00
20	"	" (TOWEL RACK)				14.50
21	8-1	RADIO SHACK (EXT. CORD)				20.00
22	8-4	CABLE CO. (BOX)			20.00	
23	8-12	PENNEY'S (BUCKETS)				12.00
24	"	" (TABLE)		45.00		
25	"	" (TOASTER)				45.00
26						
27						
28						
29						
30						
31						

(Size Reduced)

HOME-RELATED

FOOD

YEAR-DATE PAID	PAID TO:	1 GROCERIES	2 EATING OUT	3 ENTER-TAINING	4 OTHER
1-4	KROCKER'S	197.50			
1-7	STEAK & STOUT		35.00		
1-18	FOODWAY	106.00			
1-20	" (B-DAY PARTY)			45.00	
1-21	STEAK & STOUT (BUS.LUNCH)				65.00
2-1	SCHOOL LUNCHES (JAN.)				40.00
2-3	KROCKER'S	255.00			
2-6	WINDOW'S		15.00		
2-18	FOODWAY	195.00			
2-22	WINDOW'S		16.50		
2-27	STEAK & STOUT (ANNIV.)				56.00
3-1	SCHOOL LUNCHES (FEB.)				40.00
3-7	KROCKER'S	148.00			
3-18	"	190.00			
3-22	STEAK & STOUT (BIZ.)				43.00
3-24	WINDOW'S		12.50		
3-29	KROCKER'S	95.00			
4-1	SCHOOL LUNCHES (MAR.)				40.00
4-15	STEAK & STOUT		32.00		
4-16	FOODWAY	210.00			
4-20	MAC DOOGLE'S		7.00		
4-28	KROCKER'S	74.00			
5-1	SCHOOL LUNCHES (APR.)				40.00
5-4	STEAK & STOUT		35.00		
5-7	MAC DOOGLE'S		6.50		

(Size Reduced)

+-$+-$+-$+-$+-$+-$+-$+-

A MONTHLY RECORD OF BASIC HOUSEHOLD EXPENSES

HOME- RELATED

HOUSEHOLD EXPENSES

YEAR		GROCERIES	GAS	ELECTRICITY	WATER
JANUARY	1ST HALF	79.99			
	2ND HALF	133.54			
	TOTAL:	$ 213.53	86.77	57.63	26.99
FEBRUARY	1ST HALF	103.39			
	2ND HALF	145.10			
	TOTAL:	$ 248.49	265.60	49.52	23.60
MARCH	1ST HALF	126.88			
	2ND HALF	103.59			
	TOTAL:	$ 230.47	146.29	57.58	31.49
APRIL	1ST HALF	109.41			
	2ND HALF	—			
	TOTAL:	$ 109.41	122.39	46.95	28.47
MAY	1ST HALF	—			
	2ND HALF	138.81			
	TOTAL:	$ 138.81	57.94	143.65	19.21
JUNE	1ST HALF	131.88			
	2ND HALF	131.15			
	TOTAL:	$ 263.03	39.78	61.16	24.02
JULY	1ST HALF	152.08			
	2ND HALF	129.96			
	TOTAL:	$ 282.04	21.41	91.83	24.76
AUGUST	1ST HALF	158.99			
	2ND HALF	125.15			
	TOTAL:	$ 284.14	22.10	169.74	25.88
SEPTEMBER	1ST HALF	127.71			
	2ND HALF	147.83			
	TOTAL:	$ 275.54	30.41	70.43	26.25
OCTOBER	1ST HALF	157.68			
	2ND HALF	171.64			
	TOTAL:	$ 329.32	45.29	67.24	25.51
NOVEMBER	1ST HALF	142.03			
	2ND HALF	141.98			
	TOTAL:	$ 284.01	59.78	46.85	23.65
DECEMBER	1ST HALF	139.22			
	2ND HALF	150.37			
	TOTAL:	$ 289.59	112.02	63.05	24.76
YEAR'S TOTALS —		$2,948.38	$1,003.79	$859.63	$304.61

(Read across both pages.)

	TRASH SERVICE FEE	SANITARY BOARD – SEWER	TELEPHONE –LOCAL & LONG DISTANCE	NEWSPAPER				
2	15.00			33.80				
3								
4		11.89	81.49					
5								
6								
7		10.59	88.85					
8								
9								
10		9.14	202.11					
11	15.00			33.80				
12								
13		11.60	159.90					
14								
15								
16		10.15	161.54					
17								
18								
19		6.53	186.81					
20	15.00			33.80				
21								
22		8.41	130.59					
23								
24								
25		8.70	151.87					
26								
27								
28		9.14	131.71					
29	15.00			33.80				
30								
31		9.28	118.11					
32								
33								
34		8.99	136.87					
35								
36								
37		8.27	183.19					
38	$ 60.00	$ 112.67	$ 1,733.04	$ 135.20				

Section 9. Wrapping Up The System

This is the last section on the basic paper management system. Here we will introduce some refinements and adaptations to add versatility. This system is adaptable to many kinds of records and for record keeping, will function quite well in place of a home computer. It is not intended to be used for very large numbers of files but, with a little regular attention, will serve the average individual, household, and small business quite adequately.

LABELING THE LEDGER BOOKS

Even if you are using just one ledger book it is a good idea to label it. And of course, if you are using several, labeling is a must. You may acquire some self-stick 2 X 3 inch labels at most office supply stores. Write on the label the primary use of the book, such as: "Personal," "Household," "Check Ledger," etc. If you are keeping the ledger books on edge in a large desk drawer, or storing them on a shelf, place a small piece of colored tape around the spine of the book for color coding and ease in identifying one book from another at a glance.

To give your Check Ledger a professional look: enlarge a deposit slip on a copy machine, then cut out your name and the bank's name and paste them on the front of the check ledger.

A THREE-COLUMN CHECK REGISTER PAGE

GIZMO & COMPANY — PAGE 10

	YEAR DATE	CH.#	DESCRIPTION	1 PAYMENT	2 DEPOSIT CREDIT	3 BALANCE
						$1,149.30
1	1-5	223	GROSE PRINTERS	185.00		185.00
2			FLYERS	—		964.30
3	1-7		⟶		320.50	320.50
4			5 CHECKS	—		1,284.80
5	1-8	224	CASH	250.00		250.00
6			PROFIT TAKING	—		1,034.80
7	1-15	225	POSTMASTER	88.00		88.00
8			STAMPS			946.80
9	2-1	226	VIP OFFICE SUPPLY	27.20		27.20
10			" "			919.60
11	2-4		⟶		728.00	728.00
12			7 CHECKS	—		1,647.60
13	2-6	227	SPEEDY AIRLINES	325.00		325.00
14			R.T. TO CHICAGO			1,322.60
15	2-14	228	IRS	625.00		625.00
16			INCOME TAX			697.60
17	2-20	229	PACK-UP BOX CO.	45.00		45.00
18			CARTONS			652.60
19	3-2		⟶		531.50	531.50
20			6 CHECKS	—		1,184.10
21	3-4	230	BILLIE'S BAGS	75.00		75.00
22			SUITCASE			1,109.10
23	3-5		⟶		687.10	687.10
24			7 CHECKS	—		1,796.20
25	3-15	231	GROSE PRINTING	200.00		200.00
26			ENVELOPES	—		1,596.20

A FOUR-COLUMN CHECK REGISTER PAGE

(Note: tax-deductible and non-deductible columns.)

GIZMO & COMPANY   PAGE 10

			1 GIZMO PAYMENT (DEDUCT.)	2 OTHER PAYMENT (NON-DED.)	3 DEPOSIT CREDIT	4 BALANCE
	YEAR DATE	DESCRIPTION CH#				$1,149.30
1	1-5	223 GROSE PRINTERS	185.00			185.00
2		FLYERS				964.30
3	1-7				320.50	320.50
4		5 CHECKS				1,284.80
5	1-8	224 CASH		250.00		250.00
6		PROFIT TAKING				1,034.80
7	1-15	225 POSTMASTER	88.00			88.00
8		STAMPS				946.80
9	2-1	226 VIP OFFICE SUPPLY	27.20			27.20
10		" "				919.60
11	2-4				728.00	728.00
12		7 CHECKS				1,641.60
13	2-6	227 SPEEDY AIRLINES		325.00		325.00
14		R.T. TO CHICAGO				1,322.60
15	2-14	228 IRS	625.00			625.00
16		INCOME TAX				697.60
17	2-20	229 PACK-UP BOX CO.	45.00			45.00
18		CARTONS				652.60
19	3-2				531.50	531.50
20		6 CHECKS				1,184.10
21	3-4	230 BILLIE'S BAGS		75.00		75.00
22		SUITCASE				1,109.10
23	3-5				687.10	687.10
24		7 CHECKS				1,796.20
25	3-15	231 GROSE PRINTING	200.00			200.00
26		ENVELOPES				1,596.20
27						
28						
29						

COMMENT ABOUT COMPUTERS

We live in the age of computers and this author is using one with a word processor program to write this book. They are great time and labor saving devices; but in some areas, especially where a small amount of different kinds of information needs to be assembled, ledgers are more practical and much less cumbersome.

There are practically endless varieties of programs for nearly every purpose, and some are excellent. But contrary to the computer manufacturer's drum- beaters, one does not need a computer setup to balance a checkbook - or keep track of the family budget.

In comparison, the ledger book is inexpensive, small, portable, permanent and versatile - and it is operated by one of the original word processors: the pen.

ADDING THE COLUMNS

Near the bottom of most ledger pages is one or two red lines, below which totals of the page columns are written. This is the much referred to "bottom line" that tells the tale.

When a page is completed, carefully go down each column and with a calculator, add the figures and write the totals below the top red line. If a time period of entries requires more than one page, allow a space of several lines at the end of your added figures for your Grand Totals (the total of all the page totals in that period).

HOME-RELATED

HOUSEHOLD EXPENSES

YEAR		GROCERIES	GAS	ELECTRICITY	WATER
JANUARY	1ST HALF	79.99			
	2ND HALF	133.54			
	— TOTAL:	$ 213.53	86.77		
FEBRUARY	1ST HALF				
		$ 329.32	45.29	67.24	25.51
	1ST HALF	142.03			
	2ND HALF	A41.98			
	TOTAL =	$ 284.01	59.78	46.85	23.65
DECEMBER	1ST HALF	139.22			
	2ND HALF	150.37			
	— TOTAL =	$ 289.59	112.02	63.05	24.76
YEAR'S TOTALS —		$ 2,948.38	$ 1,003.79	$ 859.63	$ 304.61

TRASH SERVICE FEE	SANITARY BOARD — SEWER	TELEPHONE —LOCAL & LONG DISTANCE	NEWSPAPER			
15.00			33.80			
	11.89	81.49				
	8.99	136.87				
	8.27	183.19				
$ 60.00	$ 112.67	$ 1,733.04	$ 135.20			

EARNINGS RECORD

Even though most employed persons receive a W-2 Form before tax time, it is a sound idea to keep your own earnings and deductions records. The tax time ritual of fumbling through stacks of papers in search of payroll check stubs and pay envelopes to verify your W-2 is a thing of the past with this ledger system.

Every pay period, enter the necessary data in a ledger section labeled with the name of the company or corporation with which you are employed. Below is a list of suggested column headings:

COL. HEADINGS	DESCRIPTION
Date	Date
Notes	Notes
Basic Sal.	Basic Salary
Comm.	Commission
Gross	Gross Earnings
FWT	Fed. Withholding Tax
FICA	Social Security
SWT	State Withholding Tax
Ins.	Insurance
Save	Payroll Savings, Bonds
Other	Other Deductions
Tot. Ded.	Total Deductions
Net	Net Earnings (Take home pay)

EARNINGS RECORD

P & J Corp.

			1	2	3	4
	YEAR DATE	NOTES	BASIC SAL.	COMM.	GROSS	FWT
1	1-18	1 WEEK OFF	150.00	300.00	450.00	30.00
2	2-4		300.00	323.00	623.00	54.00
3	2-18		300.00	482.00	782.00	80.00
4	3-4	MGR'S BIRTHDAY PRESENT	300.00	373.50	673.50	64.00
5	3-18		300.00	606.50	906.50	102.00
6	4-1		300.00	782.00	1,082.00	156.00
7	4-15		300.00	717.50	1,017.50	124.00
8	4-29	CLOSED 1WK FOR REMODEL.	150.00	443.00	593.00	54.00
9	5-13		300.00	399.50	699.50	70.00
10	5-28		300.00	300.00	600.00	64.00
11	6-12		300.00	1,912.50	2,212.50	372.00
12	6-24	1 WK. OFF	150.00	80.00	330.00	15.00
13	7-8		300.00	226.00	526.00	44.00
14	7-22		300.00	372.50	672.50	64.00
15	8-5		300.00	377.50	677.50	64.00
16	8-19		300.00	232.50	532.50	56.00
17	9-3		300.00	1,242.00	1,542.00	240.00
18	9-16		300.00	422.00	722.00	76.00
19	9-30		300.00	765.40	1,065.40	102.00
20	10-14		300.00	457.00	757.00	76.00
21	10-28		300.00	475.00	775.00	82.00
22	11-11		300.00	538.00	838.00	90.00
23	11-25		300.00	699.00	999.00	118.00
24	12-9		300.00	596.00	896.00	102.00
25	12-23	OFFICE PARTY	300.00	988.50	1,288.50	184.00
26						
27						
28		YEAR'S TOTALS	7,050.00	14,110.90	21,258.90	2,483.00
29						
30						
31						
32						
33						
34						

	FICA	SWT	INS.	SAVE	OTHER	TOT. DED.	NET
1	31.72	7.32	2.50	12.50		84.04	365.96
2	43.92	12.02	5.00	25.00		138.94	484.06
3	55.12	11.00	5.00	25.00		176.12	605.88
4	47.48	13.04	5.00	25.00	5.00	160.12	513.38
5	63.76	24.06	5.00	25.00		219.82	686.68
6	76.28	25.92	5.00	25.00		288.20	793.80
7	81.74	28.98	5.00	25.00		254.72	762.78
8	41.80	11.34	2.50	12.50		122.14	470.86
9	49.32	14.22	5.00	25.00		163.54	535.96
10	44.32	9.20	5.00	25.00		147.52	452.48
11	156.88	108.24	5.00	25.00		667.12	1545.38
12	42.85	7.85	2.50	12.50		80.70	249.30
13	37.08	9.66	5.00	25.00		120.74	405.26
14	47.42	13.04	5.00	25.00		155.06	517.44
15	47.76	13.64	5.00	25.00		155.40	522.16
16	41.64	12.33	5.00	25.00		139.97	392.53
17	108.72	56.48	5.00	25.00		435.20	1106.80
18	50.90	12.48	5.00	25.00		169.38	550.62
19	75.12	27.48	5.00	25.00		234.20	830.80
20	35.36	15.94	5.00	25.00		157.30	599.70
21	54.64	16.56	5.00	25.00		183.20	591.80
22	59.08	18.66	5.00	25.00		179.08	658.92
23	70.42	24.08	5.00	25.00		243.00	755.90
24	63.16	20.76	5.00	25.00		215.92	680.08
25	90.84	40.68	5.00	25.00		355.52	932.98
26							
27							
28	1506.53	557.39	117.50	587.50		5,247.45	16,011.45

PROTECTING YOUR BOOKS

You have invested much time and diligence in the preparation and maintenance of your ledger books and they should be protected from loss, injury, or prying eyes.

Between sessions of entering information, keep them out of sight. They are your private property and no one, without your permission, has a right to look at their contents - not even the tax man, unless he has the proper legal authority.

Probably the most practical place to keep ledger books is in a drawer - in a desk if you have one - if not, some other drawer that is "private." Form the habit of always putting them back in their drawer after each entry session. In this way you will not only know where the books are at all times, but greatly diminish the chance of their loss by being accidentally thrown out or carried away. When the ledgers get to the point where they contain a good deal of information, they will actually become one of your most valuable possessions.

CONGRATULATIONS

You have now completed the task, won the battle, and banished the paper monster - hopefully for good. Remember though, in order to keep from falling into the original dilemma again, you must tend the ledgers on a regular basis. Set a time each week (or day, if you only want to spend a very few minutes), and write in the information you have decided to keep records of, as it comes along.

Keep this habit and your peace of mind will more than repay you for the effort. A famous financier once said, "An orderly desk indicates an orderly mind." Like enthusiasm, disorder is contagious - but then, so is order - and order is better.

The last two sections are not really necessary for the function of this system but they contain some knowledge and ideas you may find useful. You might even be inspired to think about starting your own business. Good luck.

+-$+-$+-$+-$+-$+-$+-4+-

Section 10. Small Business Applications

I once worked for a man who owned a music store. His desk was situated facing the center of the store, where he could watch the clerks and the customers. Aside fron the store, his fingers were in several other pies and he was a very busy man.

Along with three telephones which he would on occasion use all at once, his desk was awash with papers - in stacks and piles. Sometimes I would watch him manipulate the telephones and scrounge through the mounds of papers, and I began to notice that his callers would often tire of waiting for his free-style filing system to function and hang up. I never forgot this lesson: For the businessman, ready information is essential.

DIFFERENT NEEDS

Record keeping for a small business differs from that of am individual or home in that the needs and uses are different. The former will use the end results of the records probably monthly and yearly, while the small business owner or manager may use his records several times daily.

Then too, there is the type of information to be kept. Not only income and expenses, but records of customer sales, customer lists, inventory, advertising results, employees, projected product needs, etc. must be maintained - and in such a way as to have the information at the manager's fingertips.

REASONS FOR A RECORD KEEPING SYSTEM

Every business needs a record system that keeps its top person(s) informed of how the company is doing: how much money it is making; how much it is spending; who owes it money and how much, and for how long; who has paid and did they pay the correct amount - what is the quantity of inventory (if any); how much money is in the bank, etc.

If you have an accountant, you will have to have records to show him. If he keeps the records for you, you will want to have sufficient knowledge to be able to talk with him intelligently about the condition of the company.

Then there is the IRS. It insists that businesses keep records, but allows quite a bit of latitude as to their form. When you claim deductions for business expenses, these claims must be substantiated by your records and receipts. In case you are asked to produce them to back up your deductions and you cannot, your claim will not be allowed. <u>No records, no deductions.</u>

Last but not least, should you seek a loan from a bank or other financial institution, they will very probably want to see your records.

EASY TO USE

Your record keeping system should be accurate, up to date, and just as important, easy to use. It isn't necessary to have a complicated computer program unless you have a high volume of accounts that need to be tended, bills and reminders sent, etc. etc. If the business is small, a set of ledger books will work fine and many types of records can be kept in a multi-columned, double- page layout.

WHAT YOU NEED TO KEEP TRACK OF

Before setting up your record keeping system, have a quiet think session and figure out what kind of information you need, and also would like to have, to make your view of the company's business condition clear at all times.

Unless you have an unusual type of business, the categories mentioned earlier would make a good base to start. Information to be kept: income, expenditures, records of sales, customer lists, inventory, advertising results, employees, projected product need, etc. Of course, each of these categories would be divided into their own segments; example:

CUSTOMER SALES

Customer's name   Address
Telephone (in some cases)   Item(s) purchased
Date purchased   When delivered or shipped
Amount paid or owed   Account balance (if any)
Customer's credit rating

THE IMPORTANCE OF A CUSTOMER LIST

Of course, without customers you would have no business. Therefore, one of your most valued business possessions is your customer list. Unless you are involved in a strictly walk-in business, such as a hot dog stand or a restaurant, and you don't have a need to ever contact your customers, it would behoove you to keep a customer list.

It does not matter whether they owe you anything or not, there may come a time when you need a mailing list - to advise customers of a sale, new products, a new location, whatever. This is a valuable business tool - and keep it to yourself, (unless you want to sell it to a list broker in another area).

MANY KINDS OF SYSTEMS

Record keeping systems can range from very complicated computer programs to a few ledger books. Usually those used by large organizations are very complex - but not always. There is a trend now to simplification and cutting paper handling and filing. United Parcel Service, for example, tries to do as much communicating as it can by telephone, greatly cutting down on the amount of paper its offices handle.

METHODS FOR INCOME AND EXPENSES

There are two basic accounting methods of keeping track of income and expenses. You can use one or the other but whichever one you choose, you must be consistent and use it exclusively. These two methods are:

1. <u>Cash method.</u> In this method cash is recorded when it is **received** and when it is **spent**.

2. <u>Accrual method.</u> Here cash is recorded when it is **earned** instead of when it is received. Expenses are recorded when they are **incurred** instead of when they are paid. The cash method is the most commonly used.

YOUR CHECKBOOK

A four-column ledger book makes an excellent check register for a small business. The reason for the four columns instead of the usual three is to allow a column for checks written on the company for things that are not deductible. With this system it can be seen at a glance which is which, without having to read all the entries, as with a regular three-column setup.

Keep your business checking account separate from your personal checking account. This will save a good deal of trouble later, trying to unscramble the mess - and also, the IRS strongly prefers this separate setup.

Inside the front or back cover of this check ledger, you can attach a "pocket" made from a small heavy envelope, for holding a book of checks.

You may commpare both a three- and a four-column check ledger near the beginning of Section 9.

A FOUR-COLUMN CHECK REGISTER

(Note: tax-deductible and non-deductible columns.)

GIZMO & COMPANY   PAGE 10

			1	2	3	4
YEAR			GIZMO	OTHER	DEPOSIT	
DATE		DESCRIPTION	PAYMENT	PAYMENT	CREDIT	BALANCE
	CH#		(DEDUCT.)	(NON-DED.)		81,149.30
1-5	223	GROSE PRINTERS	185.00			185.00
		FLYERS				964.30
1-7					320.50	320.50
		5 CHECKS				1,284.80
1-8	224	CASH		250.00		250.00
		PROFIT TAKING				1,034.80
1-15	225	POSTMASTER	88.00			88.00
		STAMPS				946.80
2-1	226	VIP OFFICE SUPPLY	27.20			27.20
		" "				919.60
2-4		.			728.00	728.00
		7 CHECKS				1,647.60
2-6	227	SPEEDY AIRLINES		325.00		325.00
		R.T. TO CHICAGO				1,322.60
2-14	228	IRS	625.00			625.00
		INCOME TAX				697.60
2-20	229	PACK-UP BOX CO.	45.00			45.00
		CARTONS				652.60
3-2					531.50	531.50
		6 CHECKS				1,184.10
3-4	230	BILLIE'S BAGS		75.00		75.00
		SUITCASE				1,109.10
3-5					687.10	687.10
		7 CHECKS				1,796.20
3-15	231	GROSE PAINTING	200.00			200.00
		ENVELOPES				1,596.20

(Size Reduced)

THE CASH RECEIPT BOOK

The cash receipt book is just what it says - a book in which cash received is recorded. Tax laws require the retention of copies of sales slips for several years and actually, these can be used to show cash receipts. But this is extremely awkward and clumsy, not to mention unwieldy.

A two or three-column ledger book makes a fine cash receipt book. Put in the date received, from whom received, and the amount received, and the customer's account balance, if any.

ENTRIES IN A CASH RECEIPT BOOK

CASH RECEIPTS

4

	YEAR DATE	RECEIVED FROM=	AMOUNT
1	4-4	Midwest Co.	52.21
2	4-6	Courts Service	78.40
3	"	Branden Co.	51.76
4	"	B&T Co.	146.45
5	4-7	Bay County	53.86
6	4-8	Mountain Valley	13.16
7	"	B&T Co.	103.73
8	"	Quandry Ltd.	452.36
9	4-11	Paladin	32.32
10	4-15	B&T Co.	38.10
11	4-23	Bay County	19.95
12	"	B&T Co.	176.25
13	5-5	Midwest Co.	36.82
14	"	B&T Co.	140.70
15	"	Everett Co.	158.37
16	5-6	Mountain Valley	29.57
17	5-7	Branden Co.	34.70
18	5-8		

EXPENDITURES BOOK

All expenses that are directly related to your business operation are tax deductible. In order to verify this, it is necessary to keep an accurate record of such payments plus your cash receipts and canceled checks, should you be asked to produce them.

Your expenditure book(s) should be your main and complete record of all monies spent by your company. This record should be kept in such a way that you can readily see how much you are spending in each of several categories related to your business. These would probably include: merchandise and materials, office supplies, postage and shipping, advertising and promotion, rent or leasing of office space or property for company use, utilities, telephone, taxes, fees and licenses, office equipment and repair, books, periodicals and information (such as trade magazines, newsletters, etc.), miscellaneous, and whatever else is involved in your operation.

The categories mentioned above would require a 12-column ledger book, which is in a double-page format. You could however use an 8- or 10-column book (also double page), and use two consecutive double pages to accomodate all of your categories. An alternative to this system would be to use two 8, 10 or 12-column books, putting the most active list of categories in one book, and the less frequently entered, possibly monthly items (such as rent, utilities, etc.) in the second book.

EXPENDITURES BOOK ENTRIES

	YEAR DATE	PAID TO:		TOTAL	MDSE. & MTLS.
8					
1	10-19	Quigley Advertising		50.00	
2	10-21	Presto Stamp Co.		15.95	
3	10-22	S.S. Baker — advertising		80.00	
4	10-23	Uphill List Co. MC		163.37	
5	"	Computer Mags. (printer info)		5.30	
6	"	L-Mart		2.63	
7	"	Aid-Right		1.05	
8	"	TC Mall		1.25	
9	10-24	Aid-Right		1.57	
10	10-26	Fargo Supply Co. (equip-parts)		12.39	
11	"	Hill St. News (biz-mag.)		3.10	
12	10-28	P.O.		4.48	
13	10-29	Funnybone Systems (mkting book)		22.45	
14	"	F&M Office Supply (calendar)		3.68	
15	11-2	P.O.		6.51	
16	"	Hill St. News (biz mags.)		5.98	
17	"	Aid-Right		1.93	
18	11-3	Dept. of Commerce (info.)		7.00	
19	11-14	Jewell Photo Supply (on acc.)		20.90	
20	"	Radios Plus (cord)		4.15	
21	11-6	Novels Inc. (book)		6.95	
22	"	WT Pasteup Supplies		18.55	
23	"	Easy Print (copies)		1.68	
24	11-9	Aid-Right		.31	
25	"	Quick Print (titles & copies)		51.10	51.10
26	"	P.O.		5.04	
27	11-11	Quick Print (titles & copies)		23.30	23.30
28	11-12	Wabash Books (mkting book)		15.72	
29	"	Aid-Right		2.34	
30	"	Quick Print (copies)		15.30	
31	11-13	Tod Books		14.89	
32	11-16	UPS		17.30	
33				591.37	74.40

(Read across both pages.)

OFFICE SUPPLIES	POSTAGE & SHIPPING	ADVERTISING & PROMO.	TAXES, FEES PHONE	Books, Pxcls. INFO.	OFFICE EQUIP. & MISC.	
		50.00				1
15.96						2
		80.00				3
		163.37				4
				8.30		5
2.63						6
1.05						7
1.25						8
1.57						9
					12.39	10
				3.10		11
	4.48					12
				22.45		13
3.68						14
	6.51					15
				5.98		16
1.93						17
				9.00		18
		20.90				19
4.15						20
				6.95		21
18.55						22
1.68						23
.31						24
						25
	5.04					26
						27
				15.72		28
2.34						29
15.30						30
				14.89		31
	17.30					32
70.39	33.33	264.27		86.39	12.39	33

CREDIT CARD PURCHASES

If you make purchases for your company using a company credit card, it may be best for accuracy to enter the purchase in the expenditures book on the date purchased. Quite often your credit card purchase copy, and also the monthly statement, when it is received later, do not describe the item purchased.

TRAVEL EXPENSES

If your business involves travel, you will certainly want to keep track of expenses incurred for transportation, meals and lodging, entertainment, cab fares, tips, etc. Remember - always get receipts. There are small books printed for this purpose but any small notebook will suffice. When you get back to the office, be sure to enter this information in your main expenditures book, along with any company-related purchases made during this period.

KEEP RECORDS UP TO DATE

Form the habit of entering in the expenditures book any money paid out as soon as possible. The practice of letting items accumulate before you get around to writing them into their proper categories can cause forgetfulness and errors, and every one of these will cost you money. A help in doing this is to make such entries at the same time you write the check. Remember, log it in when it happens.

MAKING ENTRIES

Don't worry about confining your writing to the small bookkeeping-style column dividers. Use a semi-fine, black ink pen. The black ink makes better photo copies, should you need any. For the column headings, print legibly. You can make the entries below in longhand if your handwriting is clear and easy to read. Keep the entries neat, accurate, and readable. Bear in mind that errors in the entry figures will live to haunt and mislead you later. Sometimes faulty information is worse than none.

THE CUSTOMER ORDER BOOK

If you have anything to do with mail order (direct mail) sales, you will have to keep more detailed records than, for instance, a walk-in store or a restaurant, where the customer "makes their choice and pays their money." This will also require an 8- to 10-column, double-page ledger.

With some categories, one column may be used for two types of information, especially if it consists of one letter or a few digits. The categories involved here might be: date, name of customer, address, phone, percentage of discount (if any), name, code number or letter of item(s) ordered, state of inventory of this item, cost of shipping, total amount due, date billed, date shipped, how shipped, date and amount paid, balance (if any), dates of later billings, etc. Following are examples of a customer order book setup:

CUSTOMER ORDER BOOK ENTRIES

20

	YEAR R DATE T	SOLD TO: P.O. #	DISC. ↓	R T	8 MDSE.	8 SHIP
1	7-10 817	Broadwell So. Amer. 7183				
2	783	1002 First Ave, Brockton, NJ 08062	46%	1	11.97	1.19
3	7-13 817	Connere Haines 07104		10		
4	782	29 Linden St. Somerville, NJ 08877	5%		99.75	4.25
5	7-14 807	Bellen Inc. 02213				
6	782	920 Fargo Way, Rew, NV 89564	45%	2	21.95	1.44
7	7-14 807	Detten Co. NONE				
8	780	420 So. Park Rd. Cory, PA 22350	0%	1	19.95	-0-
9	7-20 807	Marsh Book Service 22350		2		
10	779	920 Azar St Bridgeport, CT 06610	45%		21.95	1.44
11	7-20 805	Municipal Hall 4225		1		
12	779	110 Center St. Rockville, ME 01210	15%	1	33.91	-0-
13	7-21 804	Michael Haines NONE		1		
14	778	RFD#2, Box 47, Dalton, ME 01210	0%	1	19.95	-0-
15	7-22 804	Farnsworth Pub. Lib. 18198		1		
16	777	620 Maple St. Cleveland OH 44142	15%	1	33.92	-0-
17	7-29 803	Barter & Co. 34570		11		
18	776	221 South St Chicago, IL 60612	55%	2	116.71	7.95
19	7-30 792	Camelot, Inc. R 213		15		
20	774	402 Memphis St, Wallingport PA 17701	55%		134.66	9.64
21	7-31 777	Union Billing 76705		10		
22	774	1200 Valley Rd, Geneva, IL 60030	55%		99.75	3.02
23	7-31 767	Baxter & Barnes 10171		50		
24	774	2120 So. Islendale, Maurice, IL 60750	55%	20	628.43	-0-
25	7-31 717	Brown & Mace 2221		10		
26	754	205 Myrtle St. Clinton, OH 43520	50%		99.75	3.81
27	7-31 707	Pacific Quality 4320				
28	754	35 Colgate Dr. Turbor, CA 90202	40%	1	11.97	1.19
29	8-1 707	Southwest Items T750		1		
30	753	1441 Church St. Brockton, MO 63040	40%		11.97	2.26
31	8-3 706	Wm. B. Hayes NONE				
32	753	20 Willow Run, Mantle, ME 01020	40%	1	11.97	1.19
33						

(Read across both pages.)

20

UNITS	DUE	SHPD.	BILD.	SHIPPED VIA	PAID DATE	AMT.	RE-BILLING 60 DAYS	
1	13.16	7-6	-----	PP	8-19	13.16		1
								2
								3
10	104.00	7-13	-----	UPS	11-9	104.00	10-1	4
								5
2	23.89	7-14	----.	PP	9-22	23.39		6
								7
1	19.95	7-14	----	PP	8-13	19.95		8
								9
2	21.39	7-20	.---	PP			10-1	10
								11
2	33.91	7-20	...	UPS	7-20	33.91		12
								13
1	19.95	7-21		PP	7-21	19.95		14
								15
2	33.92	7-22	-...	UPS	8-28	33.92		16
								17
13	124.66	7-27	.---	UPS	10-13	124.66	10-1	18
								19
15	144.30	7-28	.---	UPS			10-1	20
								21
10	162.77	7-31	-...-	UPS			10-1	22
								23
70	625.43	7-31		UPS			10-1	24
								25
10	109.56	7-31	-..-.	UPS	11-6	103.56	10-1	26
								27
1	13.16	7-31	-.--.	PP	8-13	13.16		28
								29
1	14.23	8-1	----	PP			11-1	30
								31
1	13.16	8-3	-..-.	PP	11-3	13.16	11-1	32
								33

PURCHASING

One of the first steps you will take in a new business operation is buying; probably some office furniture and equipment, etc. Do a lot of shopping and price comparing. There are some very good bargains to be had in the secondhand market, especially office furniture.

Equipment involving mechanicals or electronics, however, may be another story, since these items on the used equipment market rarely if ever have any guarantees or warranties.

Before you buy a "big-ticket" or reasonably expensive item, you not only need to know comparative prices but such things as: service on the item, quality, delivery, durability, upkeep, and possibly storage. Then there is the subject or supplies for the product, such as: continuing availability of ribbon cartridges or printwheels for printers, special papers for calculators, software for computers, etc.

And speaking of computers, most of them are fine, but <u>do a lot of "homework"</u> before buying. A rule of thumb is: figure exactly what it is you want a computer for and what you want it to do. Then find the software that will do it - then compare the computers that will run this software.

In purchasing, check alternatives. Often the wholesalers will have very low prices on an item, provided you buy a lifetime supply. Instead of taking this reckless gamble, get the quantity you require at your local office supply, or wherever.

HINTS AND HELPS

If the shipping and billing address is the same, enclose an "Invoice/Statement" <u>with</u> the merchandise. It saves time, postage, and paper work.

State "30 days net" on your Invoice/Statement, and do not let business customers run bills for over 90 days.

Do not ship merchandise to individuals until their check clears. Checks do not often bounce but the bank charges prohibit the risk.

If a customer is dissatisfied, have him return the merchandise and refund his money without a squabble. It pays.

Formulate a "discount and return" policy you can live with - and stick with it.

Allow each of the same type of customer the same discount rate. In most cases, it is the law anyway.

Keep a good credit rating: Pay your bills on time and keep a clean record at your bank. It makes a good reference.

Subscribe to at least one good newsletter in your field; but shop around. Some of these are very over-priced.

Hold employees responsible for their individual duties. Don't let "passing the buck" be a cover for incompetence.

PAPER INTIMIDATION

The idea that there is something magical about pieces of paper with writing on them is imbedded in our society. We are deluged with advertisements, reports, letters, invoices, printed forms, memos, news clippings, price quotations, computer printouts, and on and on. But by the same token, a clean desk is supposed to (but doesn't necessarily) signify an efficient executive. This steady attack of paper cam eventually become overwhelming, and inundate a businessman's desk to the point where it resembles that of the man with the three telephones, described at the beginning of this section.

In order to comply with government regulations and to provide some protection against possible law suits, certain records must be maintained. The trick in avoiding paper accumulation is to be very discriminate as to what stays and what goes. It has been said that "paperwork is the least efficient operation in U.S. industry." It might also be said that a full wastebasket indicates a good measure of success concerning this problem.

"DO WE NEED THIS?"

Keep in mind the reasons listed below, and of course other reasons tailored to your specific business. But before filing or keeping more "accumulating paper snowflakes," ask yourself: "Do we need to keep this? Why do we need to keep this? What would happen if we didn't keep this?"

Your business may require information for some or all of the following purposes:

1. To provide a customer file.

2. To meet government requirements.

3. To plan ahead.

4. To meet obligations.

5. To control your routine activities.

6. To provide protection against possible law suits.

PHONE CALLS AND NOTES VERSUS LETTERS

Many companies are now cutting down on their letter writing and letter copy accumulation by simply telephoning their customer - excluding, of course, situations where documentation is required. Telephoning instead of writing may save the exchange of several letters.

Here is another paper saving practice that is gaining acceptance: If a letter is received that does not require a formal answer, write a brief handwritten message on the face of the original letter, make a copy for your files, and return it to the writer. This gives an impression of friendliness and informality, and at the same time saves time and money.

You might add some refinements to this practice by having some small, colorful press-on labels imprinted with the company's and/or your name and a brief message at the top, to the effect: "We hope you will excuse this informality if it helps to speed our reply.

EASE AT TAX TIME

At the end of each quarter you will want to total the columns in your ledger books, (especially in the income and expenditure books) to determine your gain or loss for that period. You will also need this information for your quarterly local, state, or federal taxes (if any). The requirements here may vary as some area governments require their Business And Occupation tax to be based on gross earnings, while other areas use a base of net profit.

Allow space in each of these books for these quarterly figures to be posted, preferably just after your last entries. And of course, after the year's fourth quarter you will need space for the year's final figures.

You will find this system of keeping records makes preparing figures for your tax forms comparatively child's play. This can be especially said concerning the IRS's Schedule C form (Profit or Loss From Business or Profession), which requires the itemized figures for various categories. If you are using the system described in this book, this diversification will have already been done.

Whether you use an accountant, a professional tax preparer, or do your business taxes yourself, this recordkeeping system should be of great help. But with whatever enterprise you are involved - the best of luck.

GUIDELINES AND AXIOMS

A small business may be defined as a business that requires one "full-time" top executive.

Your most effective management tool is to always know the amount of the company's liquid assets.

A small business has to be better at management than a large business because it can't afford a large central office and a stable of specialists.

When business is going up, you never quite make as much as you think you are making. When business is going down, you nearly always lose more than you think you are losing, and at a much faster rate than you think.

Set up a system that keeps you in touch with your company's financial health and operating status.

Think especially hard before investing money in anything "new."

Doing business without advertising is like winking at a girl in the dark: You know what you're doing, but she doesn't.

Knowledge comes by taking things apart, but wisdom comes by putting things together.

Plaque on an executive's desk: "Once I thought I was wrong - but I was mistaken."

One of the great satisfactions in life is to formulate a constructive plan, then carry it out.

Intelligence is very much like money. If you don't reveal how little you have, people will treat you as though you have a lot.

Be inventive. It saves money and it's fun.

Always remember that money isn't everything. But also remember to make a lot of it before talking such nonsense.

It is good to have money and the things money will buy. But it is also good to occasionally make sure we haven't lost sighht of some of the things that money can't buy.

+-$+-$+-$+-$+-$+-$+-

Section 11. Other Uses For This System

This method of using ledger books for record keeping is adaptable to a wide variety of subjects, a few of which will be explored in this chapter. Practically any subject or project that involves ongoing figure accumulation for comparison or totaling can be set up by using the appropriate formatting and column headings. Below is a short list of some more common projects that might be set up:

Investments	Fitness
Weight Control Record	Debts
Major Medical Expenses	Lotteries
Betting	Hobby Expenses
Ideas and Inventions	Household Inventory
Savings	Personal Possessions Inventory
Shop Inventory	Moonlighting Earnings
A Pet Project	Personal Wardrobe Inventory

The above inventory-type records would be of great help for insurance purposes. (A "registered" list is usually required; check with your company.) The personal wardrobe inventory, with dates for articles purchased, would give an insight into dressing and general appearance habits, as most of us unconsciously tend to fall into redundant patterns of dress. Categories such as investment record keeping should be considered as an absolute necessity.

DATE:

7 HOME SHOP INVENTORY

	#	ITEM:	PURCHASE PRICE
1	1	Radial Arm Saw	$ 750.00
2	1	Drill Press	425.00
3	1	Belt Sander	195.00
4	1	Bench grinder & motor	65.00
5	1	Vise	45.00
6	3	Hand electric drills	85.00
7	1	Hand sander – electric	25.00
8	60	drill bits & accessories	75.00
9	1	Propane torch outfit	30.00
10	20	Screwdrivers	45.00
11	15	Pliers	75.00
12	4	Hand Saws	100.00
13	8	Clamps	40.00
14	3	Hammers	25.00
15	6	Measuring & Leveling devices	30.00
16	1	Kit of Electrical Repair tools	95.00
17	2	Soldering irons & accessories	28.00
18		Assorted screws	40.00
19		Assorted nails & fasteners	35.00
20		Adhesives, etc.	30.00
21		Assorted brushes	35.00
22		Misc. hand tools	175.00
23		Wire – assorted	50.00
24	1	Work bench & accessories	250.00
25		Assorted paint	65.00
26			
27		TOTAL	$ 2,813.00
28			
29			
30			
31			
32			
33			

KEEPING TRACK OF YOUR INVESTMENTS

This ledger system is particularly suited to keeping a track record of investments. If you have stocks or mutual funds with one of the large companies, a phone call to their automated services will give you daily updated price information on individual investments that interest you. This information may also be obtained daily from the Wall Street Journal, or weekly from Barron's.

By logging this information on a daily or weekly basis, including other relative information such as the DOW, S & P, etc., you can see at a glance how your interests are faring and better calculate trends. Investing in such things as stocks and stock-oriented mutual funds without keeping close attention to trends could be hazardous, and could be flirting with financial disaster. The system described here should help much to reduce anxiety.

Even of you don't actually invest but are just thinking about it, setting up a pseudo investment ledger and keeping score of your favorites is entertaining and very informative. This practice tracking is strongly recommended to the novice investor before he actually makes a commitment.

A two-page, 10 or more column layout is best for tracking investments. If you wish to also track many similar stocks or funds for comparison purposes, the multi-columned pads are useful and inexpensive and are available at good office supply stores. Most are provided with holes for three-ring binders.

EXAMPLES OF INVESTMENT RECORDS AND TRACKING SHEETS (below)

SHARES: 1,371.360

DATE	DOW	GROWTH STOCK:	CURRENT GAIN	CURRENT LOSS	TO-DATE GAIN	TO-DATE LOSS	CURRENT BALANCE $
8-25	-25.15	21.43	382.62		382.62		30,072.92
8-26	-20.56	21.86		205.27	177.35		29,867.64
8-27	-26.79	21.71		184.94		7.59	29,662.69
8-28	-35.71	21.52		259.59		267.18	29,403.10
8-31	+23.60	21.58	81.98			185.20	29,485.08
9-1	-51.98	21.33		341.58		526.78	29,143.50
9-2	-8.93	21.22		150.30		677.08	28,993.20
9-3	-2.55	21.15		95.64		772.72	28,897.56
9-4	-38.11	21.02		177.62		950.34	28,719.94
9-8	-16.26	20.80		300.59		1,250.93	28,419.35
9-8 UPDATE		..	—	—		—	28,524.28
9-9	+4.15	20.76		54.85			
9-10	+26.78	21.05					

DATE	DOW	GROWTH STOCK	NEW HORIZONS	NEW ERA	INT. STOCK	GROWTH + INCOME	NEW AMER. GROWTH
8-20	+40.98	21.61+.27	15.57+.20	24.50+.17	31.39+.11	15.39+.16	15.78+.14
8-21	+6.15	21.78+.17	15.64+.07	24.57+.07	31.99+.60	15.41+.02	15.86+.08
8-24	-12.44	21.73-.05	15.58-.06	24.53-.04	32.20+.21	15.34-.07	15.77-.09
8-25	-25.35	21.43+.21	15.68+.16	24.68+.15	32.10-.10	15.49+.15	15.90+.09
8-26	-20.56	21.86-.07	15.64-.04	24.64-.04	32.25+.15	15.49 —	15.86-.04
8-27	-26.79	21.71-.15	15.60-.04	24.49-.15	32.61+.36	15.34-.15	15.78-.08
8-28	-35.71	21.52-.19	15.54	24.32	32.66	15.15	15.62
8-31	+23.60	21.58+.06	15.61+.07	24.61+.29	16.35 SPLIT	15.22+.07	15.70+.08
9-1	-51.98	21.33-.25	15.52-.09	24.30-.31	16.45+.10	15.04-.18	15.60-.10
9-2	-8.93	21.22-.11	15.37-.15	24.29-.01	16.50+.05	14.93-.11	15.48-.12
9-3	-2.55	21.15-.07	15.30-.07	24.22-.07	16.49-.01	14.84-.09	15.42-.06
9-4	-35.11	21.02-.13	15.19-.11	24.08-.14	16.45-.04	14.7	
9-8	-16.26	20.80-.22					

(Read across both pages.

SHARES = 689.877

TOTAL GAIN+ or LOSS-	PURITAN FUND=	CURRENT GAIN	CURRENT LOSS	TO-DATE GAIN	TO-DATE LOSS	CURRENT BALANCE $
+382.62						
+177.35	15.11					10,000.00
-53.92	15.04		46.33		46.33	9,953.67
-373.08	14.95		59.57		105.90	9,894.10
-121.69	15.01	39.71			66.19	9,933.81
-794.07	14.89		79.41		145.60	9,854.33
-895.54	14.78		72.74		218.34	9,781.59
-1,017.52	14.74		26.46		244.80	9,755.12
-1,252.58	14.66		52.94		302.24	9,702.19
-1,732.60	14.54		79.43		381.67	9,622.76
-1,680.89	14.55	6.62				
-1,656.80	14.62					

EQUITY INCOME-	CAPITOL APPREC.	PRIME RESERVE	CASH RESERVE	PURITAN	MAGELLAN	OVERSEAS
15.23+11	12.31+05					
15.26+03	12.35+04	6.15	6.25	15.14	60.51	39.24
15.24-02	12.31-04	6.14	6.21	15.10	60.31	39.63
15.29+09	12.34+03	6.14	6.21	15.16	60.75	39.26
15.26-03	12.34 —	6.13	6.24	15.11	60.67	39.48
15.19-07	12.32-02	6.12	6.23	15.04	60.16	39.92
15.08	12.26		6.22	14.95	59.55	39.92
15.14-06	12.31+05	6.16	6.19	15.01	59.83	39.96
14.99-15	12.23-08	6.21	6.19	14.89	59.13	40.21
14.93-06	12.19-04	6.21	6.17	14.78	58.63	40.43
14.88-05	12.22+03	6.22	6.16	14.74	58.36	40.22
14.81-07	12.25+03	6.20	6.14	14.66	57.86	
14.69-12	12.17-05					

HEALTH-RELATED

Aside from what your doctor tells you about your state of health, it is good to keep your own record of such things as weight, blood pressure, exercise, nutrition, diet, etc.

Basic Data & Exercise Record:

Date, blood pressure, walked, jogged or ran (distance), exercised (time), visits to a fitness center, etc.

If you are taking dietary supplements (vitamins, minerals, herbs, etc.), it is a good way to keep a record so when you feel you need to change your "formula," this list will be a guideline.

Nutritional Supplements - Daily Doses:

(Vitamins) A, B1, B2, B6, B12, C, D, E, Etc.

Doctors, Hospitals...

Payments for doctors, hospitals, tests, and prescribed medications should also be kept in your health-related section. These will be used for tax deductions, insurance and Medicare. An example of entries for these type of records is shown at the bottom of pages 74 and 75.

FINANCIAL OBLIGATIONS

Mortgages, loans and similar obligations are another area where ledger books are ideal. You make payment, log it in the ledger, subtract the amount and write in the new balance. You always know where you stand and when the next payment is due. The same procedure can be applied to personal loans and debts, along with alimony and child support.

Here also, the compiling of these figures is not just for your personal convenience and satisfaction. Nearly all of these items are tax deductible in whole or in part and a good record should be maintained. After you have logged in your figures, be careful to file your receipts, together and in their proper place in your filing system, just in case you later have to produce them as proof of payment.

IDEAS AND INVENTIONS

Many persons have flashes of ideas about improving something: an idea for a new gadget or device - or a system for doing something better. Few people, however, know what to do with the idea after they get it. The first thing to do when an idea strikes is to write it down, lest it be lost for eternity in the void of forgetfulness. Describe the thing, idea or system you have in mind and what it does. If it is a thing rather than an idea, make a simple drawing of it, labeling the parts and what they do. This doesn't have to look professional, just so you get it on paper.

A journal-type bound book is an excellent place to keep these ideas until you can take steps to protect them. This also prevents loss, as might occur if they were on slips of paper. Be sure to date the pages containing your idea, and you might also have these pages notarized as an added precaution before taking steps to develop and promote your idea.

IN CLOSING

The author sincerely hopes this book has been of benefit to the reader and has shown a method of defense against the increasing onslaught of paper accumulation in today's world.

If you will process the papers you really need to keep on a regular basis, as suggested in this system, you will maintain control of your papers, and have one less cause for anxiety. Best wishes.

ABOUT THE AUTHOR

Charles (Jack) Bradley spent his early career as a professional musician (pianist) and toured extensively. He has also been the leader, arranger, and business manager of several bands. He is a master piano technician and has headed the piano service departments of several large music stores, plus his own piano service business. He is also an author and the founder and chief executive of a successful publishing company.

Glossary

accounting: Classification, analysis and interpretation of the financial or bookkeeping records of an enterprise.

accounts payable are current liabilities that are incurred on open credit.

accounts receivable are amounts due from customers for purchases of goods or services on an open credit basis.

accrue: To accumulate or be added periodically, such as interest.

accrued liabilities include taxes, such as: sales, payroll, and income taxes, salaries and wages earned by employees but not yet paid, and interest due on obligations of the business.

assets are resources owned by the business.

auditing: The examination of accounts by a person or persons who have had no part in their preparation.

balance: A business is always in a condition of equality or "balance". What it owns equals what it owes to either its creditors or its owners.

Balance Sheet Equation: Assets = Liabilities + Owners' Equity.

Balance Sheet: A report made by the accountant showing the condition of the firm on the last day of an accounting period. It may also be called "Operations Statement" or "Profit and Loss Statement".

bankrupt: The financial state of a person, firm, or corporation, which through a court proceeding, is relieved from the payment of all debts, after all the assets have been turned over to a court appointed trustee to protect the creditors.

capitol gain: The increase in value of an asset, such as real estate or stocks, between the time it is bought and the time it is sold.

corporation: An incorporated business owned by one or more persons.

current assets are cash and other assets that can reasonably be expected to be sold, converted or consumed in the near future through normal business operations.

current liabilities are liabilities owed to creditors that must be paid within the current fiscal period.

debit: A record of an indebtedness. A charge against a bank deposit account.

depreciation accounting: A category involving fixed assets since the life of these assets extends over many fiscal periods.

double-entry: A system of bookkeeping that requires that for every entry made on the debit side of an account, an entry for a like amount be made on the credit side of another account.

earnest money: Something of value conveyed to the seller by the buyer to bind the bargain.

equity: The money value of, or the interest in a property in excess of claims or liens against it.

executive: A person whose position calls for the making of decisions and the exercise of power over others in administering the affairs of a business or government.

fiscal period: A length of time used by a business as its accounting cycle.

fixed assets: Such items as: typewriters, machinery, land, buildings, trucks, etc.

intangibles are such things as: patents, copyrights, trademarks, franchises, and good will.

liabilities: What is owed by a business to persons or other businesses other than its owners.

long-term liabilities are liabilities that are not due to be paid in the current fiscal period.

merchandise inventory is assets that can reasonably be expected to be sold in the current fiscal period.

near future is a term generally defined as one year from the Balance Sheet date.

owner's (or owners') equity is what the business owes its owners.

partnership: An unincorporated business owned by two or more persons.

promissory note: A formal document describing amounts due from customers for purchases of goods or services and stating date payment is due and signed by the borrower.

proprietorship: An unincorporated business owned by one person.

-+-+-+-+-+-+-+-

Index

-A-

about the author	120
about this book	11
accounting	121
accounts payable	121
accounts receivable	121
account reconciliation	56
accrue	121
accrued liabilities	121
adding columns	85
appliance manuals	49
assets	121
auditing	121

-B-

bank draft	51
banking definitions	51
bankrupt	122
balance	121
balancing checkbook	55
balance sheet	122
Balance Sheet Equation	121
basic definitions	18,19
bibliography	127
bouncing checks	107
boxes	33
business filing system	30

-C-

capitol gain	122
captions	32
Cash Receipt Book	98
check	51
checkbook	96
check ledger/register	54,97
check register pages	83-84
check registers	52-54
column headings	67
computers	85
corporation	122
credit card purchases	102
credit rating	107
current assets	122
current liabilities	122
customer list	95
Customer Order Book	103

customer sales	94

-D-

debit	122
depreciation accounting	123
Discount & Return pol.	107
discounts	107
dissatisfied customer	107
dividing up pages	65
double-entry	123

-E-

earnings record	87
employees	107
envelopes	34
equity	123
earnest money	123
executive	123
Expenditures Book	99
expenses methods	95

-F-

filing	29
filing basics	31
filing cabinets	33
file folders	34
financial obligations	119
fiscal period	123
fixed assets	123

-G-

groupings	60
Guidelines & Axioms	111-112

-H-

health-related	118
Hints And Helps	107

-I-

ideas	119
identifying accounts	52
income methods	95

indexing   39
insurance due dates   73
intangibles   123
inventions   119
inventory records   113
investments   115
Invoice/Statement   107
IRS   21
item sorting list   23,24
item-type sorting   23

-J-

-K-

keeping documents   27
keeping records   16
kinds of systems   95
knowledge   16

-L-

labeling ledgers   82
ledger check register   55
ledgers spaces   66
letters   109
liabilities   123
list of illustrations   10
long-term liabilities   124

-M-

making entries   73,103
mfgrs. of ledger books   58
mfgrs. of ledger pads   58
merchandise inventory   124

-N-

near future   124
needs   20,57
newsletter   107
notes   109

-O-

overdraw   51
owner's equity   124

-P-

partnership   124
phone calls   109
plan   14
promissory note   124
proprietorship   124
protecting books   90
protecting records   33
purchasing   106
purging files   50

-Q-

-R-

record keeping systems   93
records up to date   102
reminder list   48
rules for filing   42

-S-

screening   32
setting up columns   59
sorting   22
stop-payment   51

-T-

tax time   110
terms for indexing   40
"30 days net"   107
travel expenses   102

-U-

using ledger books   59

-V-

-W-

where to find items   58
why keep records   16

-X Y Z-

+-+-+-+-+-+-+-+-+

Bibliography

Filing Systems and Records Mamagement Second Edition – College Series by Kahn, Yerian, & Stewart. C 1971, 1982. McGraw Hill Co., New York, NY

How To Become Financially Successful By Owning Your own Business by Albert J. Lowry, Ph.D. C 1981 Simon & Schuster, New York, NY

Accounting Made Simple by Joseph Peter Simini. C 1967, Doubleday & Company, Garden City, NY

Tax Guide For Small Business IRS Publication #334, (Rev. Nov. 1986). U.S. Govt. Printing Office, Washington, DC

Small Business Record Keeping by Joan Briggaman C-1983 Delman Pub. Co., Albany, NY

The Start-Up Entreprenur by James R. Cook. C 1986 E.P. Dutton, New York, NY

Successful Free-Lancing by Marian Faux. C 1982 St Martin's Press, New York, NY

Bookkeeping Made Simple by Louis W. Fields. C 1956 Doubleday & Company, Garden City, NY

The Modern American Business Dictionary by John Berenyi. C 1982, William Morrow 6 Co., New York, NY

Your Federal Income Tax: For Individuals IRS Publication #17, U.S. Govt. Printing Office, Washington, DC

-+-+-+-+-+-+-+-+-